A PAUSE TO REFRESH
DEVOTIONAL

Take Five
to overcome the tyranny of the urgent that crowds out the importance of refreshing your spirit each day and being "made new in the attitude of your minds." Ephesians 4:23

BEN FERGUSON

A Pause to Refresh
© Ben Ferguson
All rights reserved

Published by:
Ben Ferguson
1244 Rosalia Avenue
San Jose, CA 95117

Unless otherwise indicated, Scripture quotations are taken from the Holy Bible, New Living Translation, copyright © 1996, 2004, 2015 by Tyndale House Foundation. Used by permission of Tyndale House Publishers, Inc., Carol Stream, Illinois 60188. All rights reserved.

Scripture marked ESV is taken from The ESV® Bible (The Holy Bible, English Standard Version®). ESV® Text Edition: 2016. Copyright © 2001 by Crossway, a publishing ministry of Good News Publishers. The ESV® text has been reproduced in cooperation with and by permission of Good News Publishers.

Scripture marked KJV is taken from King James Version. Public domain.

Scripture marked MSG is taken from The Message. Copyright © 1993, 1994, 1995, 1996, 2000, 2001, 2002. Used by permission of NavPress Publishing Group.

Scripture marked NASB is taken from the NEW AMERICAN STANDARD BIBLE®, Copyright © 1960, 1962, 1963, 1968, 1971, 1972, 1973, 1975, 1977, 1995 by The Lockman Foundation. Used by permission.

Scripture marked NCV is taken from the New Century Version®. Copyright © 2005 by Thomas Nelson. Used by permission. All rights reserved.

Scripture marked NIV is taken from THE HOLY BIBLE, NEW INTERNATIONAL VERSION®, NIV® Copyright © 1973, 1978, 1984, 2011 by Biblica, Inc.® Used by permission. All rights reserved worldwide.

Editors: Lillie Ammann and Jan McClintock
Layout and cover: Aundrea Hernandez

Also by Ben Ferguson

    God, I've Got a Problem / Ben Ferguson.

Cover: Chaplain Brian Koyn takes a pause to refresh during 2008 deployment to Iraq. Photo used by permission.

Table of Contents

PREFACE 1
NIGHT AND DAY 3
PHONE HOME 6
EVERYBODY'S DOING IT 9
TAKE A KNEE 12
CARROTS AND STICKS 15
I'M OFFENDED 18
THE HANDS HAVE IT 21
IN THE HUDDLE 24
#THOUGHTS AND PRAYERS 27
HEART TROUBLE 30
SHOW ME 33
TURBULENCE 36
WITH EYES WIDE OPEN 39
JUST A JANITOR 42
HEART OF A CHAMPION 45
IN CASE OF EMERGENCY 48
THE FONZIE SYNDROME 51
THE APPRENTICE 54
SCARS TELL A STORY 57
LOOK THE OTHER WAY 60
YOU'LL NEVER WALK ALONE 63
CIRCLE THE WAGONS 66
THE PATCH 69
A BLACKSMITH SHOP AND FAITH: 72
IF IT WERE EASY 75
IMPOSSIBLE 78
AGAINST ALL ODDS 81
WAITING, AND WAITING, AND WAITING, AND 84
GOD WILL GET YOU 87
SECURE...INSECURE 90

IT'S NOT COMPLICATED	93
GOING IN CIRCLES	96
A FEW GOOD MEN	99
SEARCHING	102
GET ME TO THE CHURCH	105
NOT AGAIN	108
THE RIGHT QUESTION	111
GOING WITH THE FLOW	114
THE BLOOD BANK	117
STOP, THIEF!	120
I BELIEVE IN YOU	123
GOING FOR GOLD	126
WHEN YOUR WORLD FALLS APART	129
WARRIOR DOWN	132
GENERAL RULES...EXCEPTIONS	135
SPEAK TRUTH TO POWER	138
FIRST THINGS FIRST	141
TO BAKE OR NOT TO BAKE	144
I CAN'T, CAN I?	147
WE NEED TO TALK	150
THE CLOCK IS TICKING	153
FLYING BLIND	156
Special Devotions for Special Days	159
THE REST OF THE STORY	160
A MOTHER'S HEART	163
MY DAD IS	166
GRATITUDE IS	169
THE NIGHT BEFORE	172

PREFACE

The D'Arcy Company revolutionized the ad industry when their campaign for Coca-Cola changed focus from the product to the behavior of people. Their light bulb moment came when they realized people need breaks in their hustle-bustle lives…in 1929! That discovery produced a tag line for the ages: "The Pause That Refreshes."

A 1941 print ad pictures a busy man at a soda fountain (Google "soda fountain") with a glass of Coca-Cola in his hand and the pitch:

"The pause for people on-the-go. People on-the-go are never too busy to go to the soda fountain. It's a place where the hurried are glad to take a minute for the pause that refreshes with ice-cold Coca-Cola…that refreshing little stop that keeps you going. The pause that refreshes."

Millions of time-saving devices have been invented since 1929; yet the more time savers we have, we still run out of time with to-do items still undone, leaving us feeling like The Roadrunner with Wile E. Coyote in hot pursuit. We identify with the expression, "The harder I work, the behinder I get!"

Perhaps we need to rethink our priorities and ask, "Is spending a few minutes with God to refresh our spiritual batteries on our list, or do we allow the tyranny of the urgent to crowd out the important, convincing ourselves God will understand, and promise to make it up tomorrow?"

If people in 1929 needed a *pause to refresh* for *people on-the-go,* in today's world the need is critical.

The Psalmist says: "As the deer longs for streams of water, so I long for you, O God" (Psalm 42:1). "My soul thirsts for you" (Psalm 63:1). Soda fountains no longer dispense Coca-Cola for our thirst, but God invites us to grab a stool at His fountain, for that refreshing stop that keeps us going.

This series of devotionals is designed to give a pause to refresh your soul each day. Read one brief chapter, then return to it each day for a week before moving on to the next chapter.

NIGHT AND DAY

Spring 1958: Our aircraft carrier was operating under radio silence and zero running lights at night during war game exercises. One night I climbed a ladder to the 07 level, opened a hatch, and stepped out onto a catwalk, closing the hatch behind me. It was a moonless night; I couldn't see anything, but I felt the wind and heard the sounds of the ship cutting through the sea. After a few seconds I opened the hatch, stepped back inside, and closed the hatch behind me, leaving the darkness behind—going from night to day. That experience and others in our lives can help us understand basic spiritual principles.

Try explaining spiritual concepts to someone using *churchese*, and they'll need a decoder ring. Seriously, make a list of key words in *Christianspeak*, then try explaining using words all can understand. Jesus the Master Teacher explains spiritual concepts by using everyday experiences. His *Rosetta Stone* was using the familiar to explain the unfamiliar: sheep, farming, wine making, ….

First things first. The creation narrative (Genesis 1, NASB) opens: "In the beginning…darkness was over the surface of the deep and the Spirit of God was moving…" Bringing order to creation begins with darkness. "Then God said, 'Let there be light,' and there was light. And God saw that the light was good." It's no coincidence darkness is God's first priority.

"God separated the light from the darkness. God called the light day, and the darkness He called night. And there was evening, and there was morning—one day." The rhythm of all life involves God—darkness and light, day and night. God's power brings the sunrise every morning to drive away darkness.

Truth for everyday life. Every sunrise/sunset is a visual reminder of God's power. "The light shines in the darkness, and the darkness can never extinguish it" (John 1:5). Each sunrise is a reminder: light is more powerful than darkness. As the hatch opens, darkness recedes. Have you ever seen darkness shining under the door of a lighted room? Stores sell nightlights to help us see when we get up at night and sleep masks to block out light if we need to sleep during the day.

Writers, storytellers, and movies use light and dark to illustrate choices we make in the struggle between good and evil. In *Star Wars*, Darth Vader, the black-clad personification of evil, asks Luke Skywalker, Mr. Squeaky Clean, to make a choice: "Join me on the dark side."

Truth for our spiritual life. John says: "In him was life, and that life was the light of all mankind" (John 1:4, NIV). Jesus declares "I am the light of the world. Whoever follows me will never walk in darkness, but will have the light of life" (John 8:12, NIV).

We make eternal choices every day. Speaking to Nicodemus, Jesus makes the spiritual parallel to a natural event and tells us why "The Light has come into the world, and men loved the darkness rather than the Light, for their deeds were evil" (John 3:19, NASB). Daily we hear Darth Vader's whisper, "Join me on the dark side."

Looking at evil and corruption around us, we might question that "darkness can never extinguish it." We're living in dark times and may feel God has abandoned us. Israel was experiencing dark times when promised "The people who walk in darkness will see a great light; Those who live in a dark land, the light will shine on them" (Isaiah 9:2, NASB).

I chose to step from a lighted passageway onto a dark catwalk, then back into the light. We make choices between darkness and light daily, so

Choose light.

PHONE HOME

A group of aliens visiting earth fled in their spacecraft when discovered, leaving one behind. Elliot discovered the hiding alien and lured him to live with his family. ET looked out a window, pointed to the sky, and said, "Home." He constructed a device capable of making intergalactic calls and said, "ET phone home." The movie ended as he pointed a glowing finger to Elliot's forehead, said "I'll be right here," boarded a spacecraft, and disappeared. A science fiction movie can teach eternal values.

Home. We can almost feel ET's loneliness as he looks toward the sky, longing for home but not knowing when or if he might get there—a few days or a few months. We've read of the loneliness and anxiety of those stranded in foreign lands when all airplanes were grounded following 9/11. ET and the passengers know they're away from home.

As Christians, we're here on a temporary visa; our citizenship is elsewhere. Peter warns us to be careful how we live as we're "temporary residents and foreigners" (1 Peter 2:11). Paul adds "our citizenship is in heaven" (Philippians 3:20, NIV).

Longing for home. Each time ET looks up, he sees more than blue sky and clouds. In his mind's eye he visualizes home and his family, and he longs to go home. We may think God is silent or has abandoned us, but he hasn't. The Psalmist says, "The heavens proclaim the glory of God. The skies display his craftsmanship. Day after day they continue to speak; night after night they make him known. They speak without a sound or word; their voice is never heard. Yet their message has gone throughout the earth, and their words to all the world" (Psalm 19:1-4). God is never silent; every sunrise, beautiful sunset, thunder, or lightning is a reminder this world is not our home.

Phone home. Communication devices during my lifetime have gone from a phone with a tail to devices allowing communication around our world in seconds and reaching into space. Communication technology is improving at warp speed but is primitive compared to God's. His network...

** *is language sensitive.* I don't know how many languages are spoken today, but whether the call is from the US or a primitive hut in a jungle, no one will hear "Press one for...." God is multilingual.

** *is personal.* How personal is it when a recording says, "Your call is very important to us and will be answered in approximately x minutes" or "Please go to our website and solve your own problem"? God said to Jeremiah "Call to me and I will answer you" (Jeremiah 33:3, NIV). On the first ring!

** *is never down.* Open a Facebook page and that command is routed through about 100 servers in less than a minute. If you Google "heaven," 641,000,000 links on the subject are generated in .54 seconds. The enormous volume during 9/11 caused some networks to crash. By contrast, the capacity of God's server is unlimited.

*** is open 24/7.* We will never hear, "You have reached me after regular business hours. Please call back during normal business hours, or leave a message and I will return your call."

Anyone who has been stuck away from home understands ET's longing for home, but the physical illustrates the eternal as Abraham who "made his home in the promised land like a stranger in a foreign country...he was looking forward to the city...whose architect and builder is God" (Hebrews 11:9-10, NIV). God is ready and waiting for us to phone home. So go ahead.

Make the call.

EVERYBODY'S DOING IT

My oldest daughter was in second grade when she came home and announced she needed a certain kind of shoes for school. When I said, "No," her response was, "But Dad, everyone is getting them." I responded, "Not everyone is getting them, because you aren't."

She wasn't happy, but she never used that *everybody's doing it* line again. It would be nice if everyone learned to avoid it, but they don't.

Peer pressure: Herd instinct. The animal kingdom illustrates how it works. Predators looking for a venison dinner don't attack the herd but wait until one deer wanders away from the group. Once a member separates from the herd, predators attack, the herd flees, and the one outside the herd becomes dinner for predators. The lesson: Be part of the herd—being alone can be dangerous!

My daughter faced the pressure to have the right shoes throughout her youth. Teens exhibit the herd instinct—expressing their individuality by dressing exactly like everyone else. Anybody who rejects the herd is subject to isolation and ridicule; the group (herd) becomes the predator, attacking anyone who doesn't get with the accepted program.

Peer pressure is alive and well today. Are you sure? Do you watch TV, listen to radio, surf the web? On these we're bombarded with ads suggesting all the cool people have product

X and you can't be cool without it. Who doesn't want to be cool? Politicians use peer pressure to silence disagreement by saying what you believe is out of the mainstream. If you don't want to be outside the mainstream, you surrender your will to group think. Questioning someone's behavior might offend them so just keep your judgmental attitudes to yourself—don't challenge the herd.

Peer pressure: Resisting the herd instinct. Can it be done? Yes, but "Just say no" is a hard sell for teens or adults. We prefer to be told what we want to hear. King Ahab asked Jehoshaphat to join him in combat operations, but before committing, he asked Ahab to consult the prophets. He did, and all four hundred of his prophets agree: Go ahead; it'll be a piece of cake. But Jehoshaphat asks for a second opinion. "Is there not also a prophet of the Lord here?" and Ahab answered that there was. "But I hate him. He never prophesies anything but trouble for me!" (1 Kings 22). Four hundred told him what he wanted to hear; one told him the truth.

Peer pressure: Drawing a line in the sand. Pressure comes from people, possessions, or practices. Joshua addresses the pressure to worship idols instead of God, and the people declare, "No, we will serve the Lord!" (Joshua 24:21).

Pressure by people. Daniel is one of a group of captives selected for training to serve the King of Babylon. All are to eat only food from the king's kitchen, "but Daniel was determined not to defile himself by eating the food and wine given to them by the king" (Daniel 1:8). He stands apart from the crowd and God honors him.

Pressure of possessions. Jesus underscores this: "No one can serve two masters. For you will hate one and love the other; you will be devoted to one and despise the other. You cannot serve God and be enslaved to money" (Mathew 6:24). It's not the money—it's our attitude toward it.

Peer pressure may be subtle but seeks to mold us into its image in every area of life: people, practices, and possessions. Have you ever heard a parent addressing *everyone's doing it* ask a child,

If everybody jumps off a bridge, will you jump too?

TAKE A KNEE

West Point 1891: Senator Burrows told cadets, "Soldiers should not be heedless to the sentiment of their songs…I would like to see every true American, soldier or citizen, when he hears the grand notes of our national air, rise to his feet in patriotic recognition and uncover." William Dana Orcutt described the scene in *Burrows of Michigan and the Republican Party: A Biography and a History*. When "The Star-Spangled Banner" began to play, "the entire battalion of cadets responded by springing to their feet with a common impulse…followed by every person in the audience and all stood with bowed heads until the last note had ceased."

"To honor America, please stand, and remain standing for our national anthem." According to History.com, the debut performance of "The Star-Spangled Banner" at a baseball game was at the first game of the 1918 World Series. Fans attending the game between the Chicago Cubs and the Boston Red Sox were asked to stand to honor America—during World War I. It's understandable that fans get angry when players take a knee to protest various injustices. Taking a knee has historical roots, but not as a tool for protests.

Honor. We're familiar with the Knights of the Roundtable and the most famous knight of all, Lancelot. He took a knee as King Arthur tapped the flat side of his sword on each shoulder and said, "Rise, Sir Lancelot." The legend of King

Arthur and his knights is fiction, but men became knights as early as the fifth century. The honor of knighthood is still bestowed. You may recognize two men Queen Elizabeth II recently elevated to knighthood: Sir Elton John and Sir Andy Murray.

Respect. My grandson's football game began with all players standing for the anthem. Two evenly matched teams were playing hard, but late in the game everything stopped when a player on the other team was injured. All players on and off the field removed their helmets and took a knee to show respect for the injured player. For a moment, they were one team. Once the injured player received medical attention and was helped to the sideline, the game resumed.

Recognition. "When Jesus was still some distance away, the man saw him, ran to meet him, and bowed low before him" (Mark 5:6). Historical reaction to God's presence was to take a knee. "Before me every knee will bow" (Isaiah 45:23, NIV). Paul recognizes and frequently reminds us that taking a knee is an act of worship—not protest, and it is central in our relationship with God. Tim Tebow regularly took a knee on the football field following a good play. "'As surely as I live,' says the Lord, 'every knee will bow before me; every tongue will acknowledge God'" (Romans 14:11, NIV).

"That at the name of Jesus every knee should bow … and every tongue acknowledge that Jesus Christ is Lord" (Philippians 2:10-11, NIV). "I kneel before the Father, from whom every family in heaven and on earth derives its name" (Ephesians 3:14-15, NIV).

A Pause To Refresh

Old men wearing ill-fitting WWII uniforms were among the attendees at an American Legion memorial service; they were in wheelchairs, used walkers, or leaned on canes or the arms of someone younger. The service began with the entering and posting of the colors. As the colors were coming down the aisle, everyone struggled to stand as erect as their frail bodies would allow, with shoulders back. Raising gnarled hands, they saluted as best they could, holding their salute until the colors passed and were posted. Not one of these old warriors took a knee or remained seated. It's hard to imagine how anyone who saw these elderly veterans stand to honor our flag would dare to take a knee.

You may take a knee during the anthem, but we're reminded in Romans 14:10 that

"We will all stand before the judgment seat of God."

CARROTS AND STICKS

All who survive military basic training know the military frequently uses sticks rather than carrots; rewarding the one who messes up and punishing all who don't. Midway through boot camp we're all expected to march in formation without mistakes; if one gets out of step, it's stick time. The guilty faces us, and we're ordered to hold our rifle with arms extended. We're young and strong; the Springfield rifle weighs only nine pounds. Piece of cake, right? As seconds, then minutes, tick by, the rifle gains weight until we can no longer keep arms extended.

Every event we experience in life, including boot camp, is an opportunity to learn life lessons, but we frequently miss them. At the moment, our thoughts are on surviving and on payback for the one causing our pain. Hindsight allows us to look beyond the pain and anger to glean some life principles.

Carrots and sticks are necessary. The pain isn't pleasant, but it's beneficial. Those of us holding our rifles think it's necessary for the guilty, not us. After hours, we engage in corrective group therapy, allowing the guilty to share our pain. Without it, we would never function as a unit.

We're members of God's family, and discipline and training are even more important than in the military. "As you endure this divine discipline, remember that God is treating you as his own children. Who ever heard of a child who is never disciplined by its father?" (Hebrews 12:7).

Carrots and sticks make us stronger. During boot camp, companies compete with each other to earn streamers for their company flags. At graduation, the company with the most streamers is Honor Company; the negative stick therapy we received made us stronger as a unit. Company 298 is Honor Company, leading all other companies onto the parade field for graduation.

We experience hard times and may ask, "God, where are you?" or "Why me?" The answer: "But God's discipline is always good for us, so that we might share in his holiness. No discipline is enjoyable while it is happening—it's painful! But afterward there will be a peaceful harvest of right living for those who are trained in this way" (Hebrews 12:10-11). Our first reaction may be to think that God has a grudge against us, but it's not a grudge—it's strength training.

Carrots and sticks build teamwork. The young man who caused our pain is part of our team; we need him with us. Soon after fleeing Egypt, a dust cloud in the distance alerts God's people to an approaching army. Problem: Israelites don't have a standing army, so what are they to do? Joshua organized an untrained group of men to meet the Amalekites in battle. As they go out, Moses and a few men go to high ground to watch. Moses holds his staff in the air, the battle is joined, and Joshua's men are winning.

Moses's staff becomes as heavy as our Springfield rifles, he lowers his arms, and the enemy is winning. "Moses's arms soon became so tired he could no longer hold them up. So Aaron and Hur found a stone for him to sit on. Then they stood on each side of Moses, holding up his hands" (Exodus 17:12). At day's end, working together enables them to defeat a superior enemy.

My brothers and I thought Dad's discipline was just to punish us, but when we became parents, we realized it's necessary for parents to train children to respect boundaries, obey rules, and take care of each other. Likewise, God treats us as children and expects us to behave responsibly. To accomplish this, our training to become mature and responsible family members may involve both

Carrots and sticks.

I'M OFFENDED

The Duplex cartoon by Glen McCoy captures a social issue in a single cartoon: Fang, reading the paper, says to Eno, "This political cartoon offends me! It's too opinionated!" Eno replies, "Well, it *is* the opinions page!" Fang replies, "But it's not *my* opinion."

Fang's response is becoming typical as people play the *I'm offended* card to silence the opinions of others. Crowd-think singles out contrary views as hate speech or micro aggression, requiring a safe place for the offended to curl up in a fetal position. Express non-approved opinions, and the crowd will isolate you.

Truth and tradition. Tender feelings are part of the human condition, but self-appointed speech police with feelings radar set to identify any who might use potentially offensive speech are everywhere. A small restaurant erected a sign advertising their breakfast menu but was required to remove it because someone might be offended. The purpose: silence non-approved speech.

Jesus, of all people, is charged with offensive speech. In Nazareth, His teaching amazes some but offends others. The leaders challenge Him as just a hometown boy without the proper schooling. "And they were deeply offended and refused to believe in him" (Matthew 13:57). A delegation arrives from Jerusalem to challenge Him over the accepted way to wash up for dinner. His response—truth triumphs over tradition—irritates the traditionalists. His disciples think He needs to lighten up a bit and ask, "Do you realize you offended the Pharisees by what you just said?" (Matthew 15:12). God's truth isn't softened to be acceptable and may offend the elite, but it appeals to the people.

Truth and conflict. Living life as Jesus did (1 John 2:6) puts us in the sights of the speech police. The Christian message and experience involve the cross, and Paul says, "The message of the cross is foolish to those who are headed for destruction!" (1 Corinthians 1:18). Later he says we're to give "no cause for offense in anything, so that the ministry will not be discredited" (2 Corinthians 6:3, NASB). Does this mean we're to soften the message so no one is offended? No. It's not what we say, but how we say it. We're to "speak the truth in love, growing in every way more and more like Christ" (Ephesians 4:15).

Truth and consequences. I learned as a young boy that telling the truth has consequences, but consequences of not telling the truth are more severe! Jesus is rejected by many in His home town and the religious establishment; when on trial for His life, He is given an opportunity to change His story and live. He chooses death over denial.

Stephen preaches Jesus, is accused of blasphemy, hauled before the religious bigwigs, and ordered to defend himself. Moment of truth: Does he stand firm or recant? He defends the message of the cross, which infuriates the council. "They shook their fists at him in rage" (Acts 7:54). He continues until "they put their hands over their ears and began shouting. They rushed at him and dragged him out of the city and began to stone him" (Acts 7:57-58) Can't you picture these guys in their robes, ranting like crazy people?

We fret over the possible loss of our tax-exempt status while Christians elsewhere must choose: Deny Christ or die. Untold numbers choose death. How will we respond when we face the same choice? Martin Luther King Jr. said, "Our lives begin to end the day we become silent about things that matter." The message of the cross may be offensive and dangerous to our health, but

It matters!

THE HANDS HAVE IT

A friend shared an interesting conversation he had with his bride soon after they were married. He asked her, "What attracted you to me?" Feeling confident it would be his looks, muscles, or brains, he was stunned when she replied, "Your hands." Totally blown away, he asked why his hands. She replied, "They remind me of my father's hands."

Unless you're very brave, it might not be a good idea to ask your wife that question. She might say, "I don't know what I was thinking." A young child was asked, "Why did your mom marry your dad?" She replied, "My grandma said she didn't have her thinking cap on."

Profound truths are usually simple. Look at your hands—if all you see are age spots, calluses, wrinkles, or dirt under your fingernails, you're missing something profound. Now ask, "Why are my hands so important?" Our hands are the extension of who we are and are instruments of love, comfort, or discomfort. You can tell your bride you love her, but she needs a touch to verify your tell.

My friend didn't have to wonder what his bride's father was like. He saw her father's hands demonstrate his love and care for her and welcome him into the family. Ever wonder what God's hands look like? It's hard, since "No one has ever

A Pause To Refresh

seen God." How can we see the invisible? John continues in the same verse "But the unique One, who is himself God... He has revealed God to us" (John 1:18). Jesus is God's visual aid.

On His last trip to Jerusalem, Jesus attracts large crowds along the way. At one point, parents bring their children to have "Jesus...place his hands on them," but His handlers try to shoo them away. Jesus sees this, scolds them, says let the children come, and "he took the children in his arms, placed his hands on them and blessed them" (Mark 10:13-16, NIV). Jesus takes time for little people.

Jesus models God; His hands touch the eyes of the blind and the diseased skin of a leper. His hands multiply bread to feed 5,000+, wash His disciple's feet, and break bread for the Last Supper. During Jesus's farewell instructions, Phillip asks Him to show them God. He answers, "Anyone who has seen me has seen the Father!" (John 14:9). He continues and then tells His disciples that if they can't believe what He's saying, "at least believe because of the work you have seen me do" (John 14:11). Jesus is Exhibit A of God's hands.

When God wasn't visible, Jesus modeled God. Jesus isn't visible, so how can people see Him? To paraphrase a line from the feeding of the five thousand in Mark 6:37, Jesus says, "You show them what I am like." Okay, but how? "Whoever claims to live in him must live as Jesus did" (1 John 2:6, NIV). Jesus wants our hands to remind others of His hands.

A barefoot boy was looking in a shoe store window on a winter's day when a well-dressed lady stopped and asked why he wasn't wearing shoes. The little boy said he had no money, so the lady took him in the store, picked out some shoes and six pairs of warm socks, and asked for a pan of water. After she washed his feet and put socks and shoes on him, the little boy asked, "Are you God's wife?"

The little boy understood that kindness is a reflection of God. People everywhere are looking in the window of life for someone to show them what God is like. Ask yourself,

Do my hands remind them of Jesus's hands?

IN THE HUDDLE

The runner was wide open with the goal line in sight, but he took a knee on the one-yard line! The hometown crowd and coaches were understandably upset as they had no idea why he did this, but they were in store for a lesson no one would soon forget.

Keith Orr was the smallest kid on the team. He had learning disabilities and trouble with boundaries. His teammates wanted to make him feel like he belonged, but how? Between classes for several weeks, the players secretly planned and schemed how to make him feel like part of the team. With the ball on the one-yard line, the quarterback called, "Keith Special!" The team broke the huddle, one of the guys handed the ball to Keith, his teammates blocked for him, and Keith scored a touchdown!

Can anything good come out of middle school? Ask the students and community around Olivet Middle School, and you'll hear a resounding "YES!" One player summed up the impact when he said, "I kind of went from being somebody who mostly cared about me and my friends to caring about everyone and trying to make a difference in everyone's day and everyone's life."

After reading this story, I wonder how many of our faith communities operate with a spiritual middle school mindset—

A Pause To Refresh

it's all about us. We gather week by week in our holy huddle to be nurtured, totally oblivious to a Keith sitting near us in need of a look, a word, or a touch as we rush by them on the way to our next Bible class or to lunch.

Jesus is never in a rush and never misses opportunities to touch the broken bodies and wounded spirits of those He encounters, leaving an example for us. His handlers think He's too busy or important for some children and they try to keep them at a distance, but Jesus says, "Let the children come to me" (Mark 10:14). Jesus takes time to teach them and us that no one is too small or unimportant to be worth His time.

Touching a leper makes a Jew ceremonially unclean, so the crowds around Jesus step back as a leper approaches, kneels, and says, "Lord, if you are willing, you can heal me and make me clean" (Matthew 8:1-2). The crowd is shocked into silence as Jesus reaches out and touches the leper and says, "I am willing. Be healed!" (Matthew 8:3). What a story to tell! But Jesus tells him to not talk about it, but to go show himself to the priests, and let them see he is healed as a public testimony.

Jesus said we're to follow His example and get out of our holy huddle—give food and drink to the hungry and thirsty, invite a stranger in for the night, clothe the naked, care for the sick, and visit those in prison who are the least among you (Matthew 25:31-40).

Following a general audience in St. Peter's Square, Pope Francis was approached by a man severely disfigured with neurofibromatosis, who asked for a blessing. Individuals with this disease are shunned, but Pope Frances stunned everyone by immediately embracing the man, kissing his head, and blessing him.

The football players at Mt. Olivet Middle School broke the huddle and changed a community. The pope left his holy huddle and touched the untouchable. Those needing a touch are outside our holy huddle. We won't make a difference until we

Break the huddle!

#THOUGHTS AND PRAYERS

We're experiencing another change in attitudes toward God and the practice of faith. How many times have we heard a report of an individual or group tragedy and hear a commentator say, "We're sending our thoughts and prayers." Although it sounds like a cliché, I don't recall it being attacked—until now.

Following the church shooting in Texas, the political class openly bashed these expressions, saying in effect, "We've banned God from the public square. Now you shut up and keep any faith to yourself." Representative Paul Ryan said the people of Texas "need our prayers right now" and was chastised by Khary Penebaker, who said, "You're paid … to act & legislate, not for your #ThoughtsAndPrayers." Governor Cuomo of New York told us to outsource prayer to the professionals: "We have pastors, priests, and rabbis to offer thoughts and prayers."

Prayer is personal. "Prayer is not a refuge for cowards." It's where we "partner with God for good" (Right Reverend Robert Wright). Forget the critics and learn what Jesus did when a Roman Centurion comes with a request for a young boy who "lies in bed, paralyzed and in terrible pain." The soldier asked Jesus to send His thoughts and prayers. "Then Jesus said to the Roman officer, 'Go back home. Because you believed, it has happened.' And the young servant was healed that same hour" (Matthew 8:6-13).

Prayer is our refuge. An injured child runs crying to mother who wraps her arms around him, wipes away the tears, and holds him close where he feels safe. God is our safe place: "The name of the LORD is a strong fortress; the godly run to him and are safe" (Proverbs 18:10). "And because we are His children, God has sent the Spirit of His Son into our hearts, prompting us to call out, 'Abba, Father'" (Galatians 4:6).

We're never promised a tragedy-free life, but we are promised we don't stand alone. Jesus said, "Come to me, all of you who are weary and carry heavy burdens … you will find rest for your souls. For my yoke is easy to bear, and the burden I give you is light" (Matthew 11:28-30).

Prayer is our comfort in troubled times. Politicians believe we should turn to them in times of tragedy rather than praying, but their track record isn't good. Jesus shares hard truth with his disciples and many turn away. Turning to His inner circle, He asks, "Are you also going to leave?" Simon Peter replied, "Lord, to whom would we go? You have the words that give eternal life" (John 6:67-68).

Two days after the church-shooting tragedy, the lieutenant governor of Texas put things in perspective and offered hope to the community when he said, "An entire church went to heaven together on Sunday morning." During very troubled times a prophet told the nation, "Those who trust in the LORD will find new strength. They will soar high on wings like eagles. … They will walk and not faint" (Isaiah 40:31).

Ravi Zacharias said tragedy is "the boomerang of sin, and the only way to stop it is at the foot of the cross." The story is told of an old woman who was walking along the road with a huge bundle of sticks on her back when a truck stopped, and the driver invited her to get in the back with others. She got in, and the truck went down the roadway. Before long, someone suggested the woman lay her bundle of sticks down. She responded, "Oh no, it's enough he's carrying me. I can't expect him to carry my bundle of sticks." We're invited to bring our burdens to the cross and

Leave them there!

HEART TROUBLE

Some friends think I was born before dirt—not quite, but dirt was relatively new. By today's standards, life was primitive. When I was born, electricity hadn't yet come to our farm; telephones didn't fit in a pocket and had a tail; TV had no color, no remote, no mute, and no DVR. Apples came from trees; we didn't ask Siri anything; texting while walking or driving wasn't a problem; communication was face to face or snail mail, not smoke signals. Knowledge of our world came from books, Saturday newsreels, radio, or someone who had traveled to faraway places like California.

A popular weekly radio program began with eerie music, then the question: "Who knows what evil lurks in the hearts of men?" More eerie music, then the answer: "The Shadow knows!" Fast forward a few decades, and we no longer ask the question. Evil is beamed into our homes on the big screen and in vivid color. We're repulsed by the new ways people devise to express their evil. We ask, "Can it get any worse?" but the right question to ask is "Why?"

God's diagnosis. We step into God's examining room, and He asks, "What are your symptoms?" We begin describing what we're seeing, but we're told those are expression of a disease, and again we're asked, "What are the symptoms?" He opens His *GDR (God's Desk Reference).* "Cursed are those who put their trust in mere humans, who rely on human strength and turn their hearts away from the Lord" (Jeremiah 17:5). Jesus says, "What you say flows from what is in your heart" (Luke 6:45). Finally, Solomon adds, "Guard your heart ... for it determines the course of your life" (Proverbs 4:23).

God places His stethoscope on our chest and says, "Breathe deeply." Diagnosis: We have a heart problem. How bad is it? "The human heart is the most deceitful of all things, and desperately wicked. Who really knows how bad it is?" (Jeremiah 17:9).

God's patience. When a doctor diagnoses a heart problem, depending on the severity, he may recommend lifestyle changes like diet and exercise before surgical intervention. God says we have a heart problem and allows us time before intervention. Abraham is promised the land of Israel, but after years the deed hasn't been recorded. He asks God, "When?" and God says it'll be four generations before the current occupants will be evicted and "your descendants will return here to this land, for the sins of the Amorites do not yet warrant their destruction" (Genesis 15:16).

God's solution. A fifty-four-year-old man was near death with a diseased heart when Dr. Christian Barnard made an offer the patient couldn't refuse—a new heart. On December 3, 1967, the first heart transplant gave him a healthy heart and a new life. The world celebrated the historic event, but God has been in the transplant business since Eden. Speaking through Ezekiel, God says they have a heart problem and makes an offer they can't refuse: "I will give you a new heart ... I will take out your stony, stubborn heart and give you a tender, responsive heart" (36:26).

Barnard later wrote, "For a dying man it is not a difficult decision because he knows he is at the end." We have a similar offer; ask and we'll receive a new heart. David, a man after God's own heart, tells us how to maintain spiritual heart health. After failure, he confesses to God, then asks, "Create in me a clean heart, O God. Renew a loyal spirit within me" (Psalm 51:10). The question is

How's your heart?

SHOW ME...

In the "old" Navy, between wooden ships and nuclear power, (1956–1958), I was a yeoman administrator with an aviation squadron. In addition to the daily duties, I prepared the weekly, monthly, and quarterly reports for the Admin Officer. After about a year, Lieutenant Gudal, our new Admin Officer, called me into his office to question whether a report on his desk was done properly. When I assured him it was, he leaned back in his chair, smiled, and said, "Show me!" I show him the regs. He said, "You're right; I'm wrong" and never questioned me again.

Lieutenant Gudal taught a nineteen-year-old Texas farm boy a valuable life lesson: "If you can't show me, don't tell me"— the opposite of "Those who can't, teach." The best teachers are those who teach from their experience, not from their reading.

A worldwide movement begins when an unknown rabbi observes two professional fishermen at work and calls, "'Come, follow me, and I will show you how to fish for people!' And they left their nets at once and followed Him" (Matthew 4:19-20).

Jesus shows them: "He appointed twelve, so that they would be with Him and that He could send them out" (Mark 3:14, NASB). The twelve are in a three-phase internship. Phase 1: "Be with Him" 24/7, observing how He engages both friendly and hostile people, breaks protocol by touching the unclean, violates rules of Sabbath rest. Phase 2: TDY (Temporary Duty). "Send them out" to practice what they've learned at His side; after-action reports indicate it goes well, indicating they're ready for deployment (Luke 9:10). What now?

Graduate school. Phase 3: Plans for key posts in the family business hit a snag; joy and anticipation turn to terror as Jesus is arrested and charged with treason. Former cheerleaders now demand His execution, a reluctant judge relents, and disciples go underground.

They're in shock and disbelief. When women report that Jesus is alive, Thomas says, "Unless I see the nail marks in His hands and put my finger where the nails were, and put my hand into His side, I will not believe" (John 20:25, NIV). Jesus shows up. Done!

An additional forty days of intensive training before He turns over the family business to them: "You will be my witnesses in Jerusalem, and in all Judea and Samaria, and to the ends of the earth" (Acts 1:8, NIV). How did they do? Of the original twelve, one was a traitor and committed suicide, ten died as martyrs, and one lived out his life in exile—but the family business went global. Now what?

Jesus sends us. The internship program continues. Young Timothy travels with Paul as he shows him how God's business operates. Once Timothy is on his own, Paul reminds him what ministry success requires: "And the things you have heard me say…entrust to reliable people who will… teach others" (2 Timothy 2:2, NIV). Paul's ministry allows him to visit many judges, jailers, and jails, including the big one in Rome.

Hostility to Christ's message of the cross was brutal in the first century and continues unabated in our so-called civilized world. Efforts to shut down God's business, the church, continue with the brutal execution of many around the globe who refuse to deny Christ. We've not experienced it on our shores, but worldwide TV images bring its brutality to screens in our homes. Will it come to our shores? Only God knows, but one thing is certain: we too are sent. "As the Father has sent me, so I am sending you" (John 20:21) hasn't been rescinded. The Church has been

In business under the same management since

Pentecost!

TURBULENCE

The flight to Dallas-Fort Worth was smooth until the final approach, when the plane started bouncing violently. The pilot informed us we were landing with a fifty-mile-an-hour crosswind. I was thinking, "Abort, Abort," as out the window I saw the ground, the sky, and the ground, until the tires hit the runway hard, bouncing down the runway to a stop. The landing was safe but not smooth!

Anyone boarding a plane expects a smooth flight and landing; if told ahead of time to expect extreme turbulence or a hard landing, many would opt out. The life of faith is a lot like boarding a flight; we expect a smooth journey and a safe landing. The problem is our expectations aren't always met, and we experience extreme turbulence in life.

Why Not Me? It doesn't take a Bible scholar to realize Jesus dispels the notion of safe spaces for His followers. He says God "gives his sunlight to both the evil and the good, and he sends rain on the just and the unjust alike" (Matthew 5:45). Later the disciples hear, "The time is coming…when you will be scattered.… Here on earth you will have many trials and sorrows" (John 16:32-33).

We have a twisted sense of the trials and sorrows Jesus talks about. Speaking to a New Jersey group of Catholic lawyers and judges on March 15, 2017, Supreme Court Justice

A Pause To Refresh

Alito warned of hostile winds ahead for religious freedoms. The threats come from an increasingly secular society trying to force conformity to a worldview without God, to silence Christians, and to take away cherished perks like tax-exempt status and the right to practice our faith without government interference. For these indignities we want...

Witness Protection. A witness with information critical to an upcoming trial whose life is in danger may be put in a witness protection program, getting a new identity in an undisclosed location. Search the Scriptures and no such program is available for believers whose life, liberty, and property are threatened by the force and might of the government. What we're experiencing in the US is the tip of the iceberg of persecution experienced around the world.

Jesus experiences suffering; His disciples experience it and are told they ain't seen nothing yet! His words: "If the world hates you, remember that it hated me first. ... I chose you ... so it hates you. ... Since they persecuted me, naturally they will persecute you" (John 15:18-20). "The time is coming when those who kill you will think they are doing a holy service for God" (John 16:2). Christians have been the target of persecution since Jesus's earthly life. We're shocked to see such hatred and barbarity overseas, but it will come to us.

Promise. One must be blind to reality to ignore Jesus's words about hate, persecution, and trouble for His followers. It's real and is increasing, but we're on the winning team. "Take heart, because I have overcome the world" (John 16:33). And we're not alone: "I am with you always, even to the end of the age" (Matthew 28:20). We will face turbulence on our faith journey but

We will land safely.

WITH EYES WIDE OPEN

We planned to leave San Diego in time to miss the rush hour traffic through Los Angeles, but when we arrived at eleven in the morning, traffic was six lanes across, going seventy MPH, bumper to bumper! I was in a middle lane, with white knuckles and a heart rate of about two hundred. If ever there was a time I needed to pray, that was it. But I needed my eyes wide open, both hands on the wheel, and total concentration on the road—no time to pray!

When our stress meter is on red alert, it's hard to remember that prayer is a conversation with God as a father. We have a check list: folded hands, closed eyes, bended knee, and formal voice and words. Jesus said, "This is how you should pray": focus on content, not phrases, position, or place to pray (Luke 11:2).

Prayer isn't a Twitter message or status post on Facebook. It's a conversation, speaking to God and listening for His response. God speaks languages other than King James English! Imagine talking to your own father the way we've learned to talk to God our Father. Had I talked to my dad the way some come to God, he would have thought I needed psychiatric care. But how can we talk to God?

During one service the worship leader was to lead us in prayer. The lights were dimmed, and all was quiet when the silence is broken with, "Hey God!" I don't remember the rest of his prayer; I looked up expecting to see a pile of smoking ashes on the platform.

If I had ever taken that tone with my dad, I'd probably still be flying through space. God is our Father, not our buddy!

Does "The fear of the Lord is the beginning of wisdom" (Proverbs 9:10, NASB) mean we should approach God with fear and trembling? No! Consider Eden; Adam and Eve have close fellowship with God without any fear, but when they break a command, "they hid from the Lord God among the trees. Then the Lord God called to the man, 'Where are you?'" Adam answered, "I heard ... so I hid. I was afraid" (Genesis 3:8-10). An alternate translation of the Proverbs passage is this: "Wisdom begins with respect for the Lord" (NCV). The only time to approach God with fear is when we've broken His law.

I never approached my dad as a buddy, and I had total respect for him. We talked every day, and I was never afraid unless I had done something wrong—whether he knew of it or not. I believe God wants us to have that kind of relationship with Him.

Back to the freeway example and praying with our eyes open. Everything is going great for Peter as a water walker until he looks at the waves instead of Jesus and is terrified. With no time to fold his hands, get on his knees, find his religious voice and the proper words and right time, he shouts, "Save me, Lord!" (Matthew 14:30).

Can we pray without using words? Yes. Otherwise, "Never stop praying" (1 Thessalonians 5:17) makes no sense.

A Pause To Refresh

God knows our hearts and thoughts (a sobering fact), and prayer is an attitude. When we're speechless and "don't know what God wants us to pray for… the Holy Spirit prays for us with groanings that cannot be expressed in words. And the Father who knows all hearts knows what the Spirit is saying, for the Spirit pleads for us believers in harmony with God's own will" (Romans 8:26-27).

We can pray in heavy traffic, during a job interview—any place, any time, in any position, and yes, we can pray

With our eyes wide open!

JUST A JANITOR

Bill Crawford moved slowly, sort of shuffling as he went about his chores mopping and buffing floors, cleaning toilets, and picking up after 100 young men in the dormitory at the Air Force Academy. The cadets went about their daily activities, barely noticing him, as he worked to keep the dorm spotless. Cadets were too important to pick up after themselves; soon they would become officers and gentlemen by an act of Congress, but Bill would still be just a janitor!

One Saturday, Cadet Moschgat was reading about a battle on Hill 424 near Altavilla, Italy, in 1943. After his retirement as a colonel, he wrote about the experience in the March 2012 issue of *Officers Christian Fellowship*. "In the face of intense hostile fire...with no regard for his personal safety, and on his own initiative Private Crawford..." stopping him cold. He showed it to his roommate, and they could hardly wait until Monday to show Bill, who quietly said, "Yes that was me." Bill was more than a janitor; he was a Medal of Honor winner!

We judge by what we see. Israel clamors for a king like the other nations and is given Saul, "the most handsome man in Israel—head and shoulders taller than anyone else" (1 Samuel 9:2). God tells Samuel to anoint one of the sons of Jesse as Saul's replacement. When he sees the first son, he thinks "Surely this is the Lord's anointed!" Nope; second son, nope;

third son, nope. Seven sons are rejected when Samuel asks, "Are these all the sons you have?" No, but David is just a shepherd (1 Samuel 16).

Jesus returns to his hometown and is teaching in the synagogue when the elders ask who does He think he is? They've known him since childhood, and "He's just a carpenter. ... They were deeply offended and refused to believe in him" (Mark 6:3).

God judges by who we are. God gives Israel a looker in Saul, who is tall and handsome. But when the chips are down, he fails "because you have not kept the LORD's command" (1 Samuel 13:14). Choosing based on looks doesn't work out because "The LORD doesn't see things the way you see them. People judge by outward appearance, but the LORD looks at the heart" (1 Samuel 16:7). David is more than "dark and handsome, with beautiful eyes" (1 Samuel 16:12), he's "a man after my own heart. He will do everything I want him to do" (Acts 13:22).

Imagine being a fly on the wall observing Jesus's frequent encounters with the religious wordsmiths. They challenge His teaching, He answers, and they declare He's demon possessed. Not playing by their rules, He breaks the Law of Moses, and He says, "Look beneath the surface so you can judge correctly" (John 7:24).

The shortest distance between Jerusalem and Galilee in Jesus's day isn't a straight line through Samaria. Samaritans are considered racially and religiously unclean by Jews who take a longer route around to avoid any contact. Jesus ignores tradition and travels through Samaria for a noon appointment with an outcast woman who needs to know God loves her, not for what she does but for who she is.

When those cadets learned Bill was a Medal of Honor winner, they treated him differently, invited him to squadron functions, spoke to him daily, and lightened his load by picking up after themselves. Bill was no longer just a janitor—he was one of them!

We go about our busy lives, and like the cadets, we unconsciously judge people for what they do rather than who they are. They're just a clerk, cook, mechanic, businessman, or housewife. Like Bill, everyone we encounter is more than what they do. Remember, each is

One for whom Jesus died!

HEART OF A CHAMPION

Athletes train hard for each competition, whether it's a high school track meet or the Olympics, the ultimate in competition. Do Olympians train year-round for years and go through tough competition just to get to the big stage? No! They train to win. I have yet to see an interview with an Olympian who said, "I'm just proud to be here."

Paul says, "In a race everyone runs, but only one person gets the prize. So run to win!" (1 Corinthians 9:24). I wonder if we haven't taken "So run to win" so literally that every aspect of life is a competition. Perhaps this is how we developed a win-at-any-cost mentality, including elbowing a neighbor out of the race. Has it ever occurred to you that it's possible we can win by losing?

Meghan Vogel, a seventeen-year-old high school student, was competing in the Ohio State Championship track meet. An hour after completing a one-mile run with a personal best, she lined up for a two-mile race. She was tired and in last place when she caught up with a competitor, Arden McMath, who was exhausted. Her legs were cramping, and she had fallen a couple of times. Instead of running past her to avoid a last place finish, Meghan put Arden's arms around her shoulders and carried her thirty meters as the crowd erupted. When they got to the finish line, Meghan pushed Arden across before her, winning even though she came in last. Meghan displayed the heart of a champion, winning by losing.

A Pause To Refresh

In our drive to win, do we take notice of others ahead who have fallen down, giving us a chance to get ahead? I know we may never see a person lying by the roadside wounded and bleeding as in the story of The Good Samaritan, but how many times do we see someone standing by the road holding a cardboard sign asking for help and drive by, avoiding eye contact? Do we have a neighbor who is hurting and in need of God's touch, but we don't want to get involved?

Those expecting Jesus to arrive for dinner at a given time are usually disappointed. He stops and helps anyone who has fallen down. Dinner is less important than one in need. He talks about caring for the hungry, thirsty, sick, and those in prisons, then He shows us how. They ask, "When did we do these things?"

He replies, "'Whenever you did one of these things to someone overlooked or ignored, that was me—you did it to me'" (Matthew 25:40, MSG).

We came out of church late, hurrying to meet someone for lunch. On the way to our car, parked where I don't usually park, we walked by a ninety-four-year-old man waiting patiently by the driveway. After putting my things in the car, I returned and asked him if he needed a ride. He said, "Yes." His son had apparently forgotten to come for him. At that point helping the man was far more important than meeting friends on time. We gave someone forgotten a ride home, and every time I see him he says, "I'm happy to see you." How many people coming out of church walked past the man who had been forgotten? Would you have stopped? Try it—you'll like it.

"Don't forget to show hospitality to strangers, for some who have done this have entertained angels without realizing it!" (Hebrews 13:2).

Ask yourself

Is the heart beating in my chest one of a champion?

IN CASE OF EMERGENCY

The platform document became an issue at the 2012 Democratic National Convention—God was excluded. During debate, a motion was made and seconded to put God in the document as in prior years, a change requiring a two-thirds majority vote of delegates. The first voice vote failed, a second vote wasn't any better, and the chairman's declaration, "Motion passed" was greeted with loud boos, surprising many delegates and a national TV audience. Why were so many surprised?

The omission and booing of God reflects not-so-subtle efforts to remove God from our city square and public life under the guise of "separation of church and state" or to avoid offending someone. Consciously or not, God's role has been reduced.

Ceremonial: The president addresses us with a list of things he wants to do, then ends with "God bless the United States of America" or "God bless our mess!"

FEMA's Backup. Stay out of sight and out of our lives. Don't call us—we'll call you when something like Hurricane Sandy devastates the Northeast coast. Before the wind and flooding ended, we heard: "Where's God when we need him? Why did He allow this to happen?"

Our founders understood "Blessed is the nation whose God is the Lord" (Psalm 33:12, NIV). They acknowledged our dependence on God, asked His blessing on our nation, placed *In God we trust* on our money, and later we added *One nation under God* to our pledge. National blessings we've enjoyed came from our dependence on God; independence removes God's blessing.

The drifting away from Judeo/Christian principles and our Biblical anchors jeopardizes our nation's future. History provides clues that are both good and bad. God's law to Israel includes the carrot (blessings) as well as the stick (consequences). One discussion ends with "But if your heart turns away and you refuse to listen, and if you are drawn away to serve and worship other gods, then I warn you now that you will certainly be destroyed" (Deuteronomy 30:17-18).

The Bad. The book of Judges records a sad yet instructive chapter in Israel's history with a recurring theme: "In those days Israel had no king; all the people did whatever seemed right in their own eyes" (Judges 21:25). After Joshua's death, "another generation grew up....They abandoned the Lord, the God of their ancestors.... He turned them over to their enemies...just as He had warned" (Judges 2:10-15).

The lesson is simple. God wants a little less talk and a lot more action! Don't ask God to bless America, and then ignore Him in our personal and national lives. "When people do not accept divine guidance, they run wild....Words alone will not discipline a servant; the words may be understood, but they are not heeded" (Proverbs 29:18-19).

The Good. In counterbalance to the judgment Israel experienced when they went their own way, God, as a father, was waiting to restore them. "When they cried out to the LORD...

the LORD sent a prophet" (Judges 6:7-8). Throughout Israel's history God raised up prophets to call His people back to Him. Not all were welcomed for pointing out rebellion against God.

Our history includes the Great Awakening when God raised up preachers who called us back to Him. For more than a half century, God's conscience and voice to presidents and our nation was Billy Graham. Now that he is no longer with us, it seems no one is filling his role as God's voice in a critical time. We push God aside, then ask "Where's God?" when bad happens. The question we should be asking is, "Where are we?" Remember

God hasn't moved...we have!

THE FONZIE SYNDROME

Each cast member of "Happy Days" brought a unique perspective and personality to the show but none more so than Fonzie—the king of cool. When we think of The Fonze, probably the most enduring image is his struggle to admit he was wrong. His attempts brought laughter but expose a deep flaw in humanity—the difficulty in admitting a wrong.

Admitting wrongdoing opens the door for several consequences—none pleasant: 1) punishment for the wrong committed, 2) a hit to our carefully constructed image, and 3) possible rejection. Fonzie epitomizes the fear of rejection by those who love us.

When God confronts Adam and Eve, they don't deny what happened. However, they try to avoid blame by passing the buck, claiming it's not their fault. Adam says, "'It was the woman you gave me who gave me the fruit, and I ate it'" (Genesis 3:12). What a guy! Not to be outdone, Eve adds "'The serpent deceived me…. That's why I ate it'" (Genesis 3:13). Their efforts to shift the blame don't prevent consequences—before sundown they're homeless.

We hear of people who pad their resumes, claiming accomplishments not earned. They may fool us but can't fool God, and He's not amused. A man named Ananias sells some property, keeps part of the proceeds—which is okay, and brings the rest to the church, pretending he's giving all. Peter questions him about it, but Ananias repeats the lie, prompting Peter to say, "You weren't lying to us but to God!" (Acts 5:4). Consequences are swift and deadly; he's buried before sundown. His wife comes in, repeats the same lie, and joins Ananias at the cemetery.

At times, my dad would tell me, "I'm not punishing you for what you did but for lying about it."

The unanswered question is this: Had Adam and Eve confessed, would they have been evicted from Eden? Had Ananias told the truth, would he have lived to collect Social Security? Had I not lied to my dad, would I have been able to sit down? In considering these questions, we have three things to guide us:

The heart of God: He comes to the garden like a Father with His arms outstretched, seeking fellowship with those created in His image. Their disobedience is a problem, but not accepting responsibility is a bigger problem. God knows what they did, and I believe He comes to the garden seeking confession and restoration—not condemnation. God's message to a rebellious nation was, "I desire mercy and not sacrifice" (Hosea 6:6, NIV).

The grace of God: The Bible is a story of love and redemption for imperfect humans. David is called a man after God's own heart, so he must have been a goody-two-shoes, right? Nope. He takes the wife of one of his soldiers, and then sees to it the soldier dies in battle. When confronted by the prophet Nathan, he cries out "Have mercy on me, O God, because of your unfailing love" (Psalm 51:1).

The forgiveness of God: "Because of your great compassion, blot out the stain of my sins. Wash me clean from my guilt. Purify me from my sin" (Psalm 51:1-2). "If we confess our sins to him, he is faithful and just to forgive us our sins and to cleanse us from all wickedness" (1 John 1:9).

Forgiveness doesn't come when we pull a Fonzie, but when we own up to wrong, we'll experience the heart, grace, and forgiveness of God. Try it—you'll like it.

Don't be a Fonzie.

THE APPRENTICE

I came home from ag class one afternoon and announced, "According to the textbook, it's time to plow the corn." Dad replied, "Son, we plow the corn when it needs to be plowed, not when the book says it does." He had been a farmer all his life, learning from his dad, and was passing on to his sons what his dad and experience taught him. He said a lot of things to us, but he never said, "You're fired!"

Following military service, one of my brothers became a machinist. He started a specialty machine shop in his garage, and the business grew and expanded. Two of his sons began working with him, not as supervisors but as apprentices—cleaning the bathrooms, sweeping the floors, and spending hours by his side at the lathes. They learned the trade and how to run the business. Following his death, the sons who learned at his side continue to run the business.

During my lifetime, the shift away from apprenticeships and job training to college degrees has produced a lot of very smart people who can't change a tire or build anything. Expensive machines often sit idle for lack of trained workers, and work is outsourced to countries who train workers. Apprenticeships are a product of ancient history and teach important lessons.

Preparing to lead. The Israelites are nearing the end of a forty-year commute from Egypt to their destination on the other side of a raging river, and there's no Golden Gate Bridge to get across. Moses, their leader for forty years, is absent, and all questioning eyes are on Joshua. Now what? Try to imagine Joshua's feelings when God says to him, "Moses my servant is dead. Therefore, the time has come for you to lead these people…across the Jordan River into the land" (Joshua 1:2). The good news: Joshua has seen God's work up close and personally for forty years as Moses's apprentice—he's prepared to lead. The bad news: He's seen the complaining and challenges to Moses's leadership, but now the buck stops with him!

Check on progress. A group of men have been observing Jesus closely for a couple years. Now it's time for a check on their progress, so their instructor begins, "sending them out two by two, giving them authority to cast out evil spirits" (Mark 6:7). How long they're away from the watchful eye of their teacher is unknown, but when they return, "they told Him all they had done and taught," which must have made an impression as the crowds were so big they "didn't even have time to eat" (Mark 6:30-31).

Training is never complete. Remaining proficient requires continuing education to maintain a level of competence. Paul travels throughout the ancient world preaching, creating scenes, getting acquainted with the inside of jails, establishing house churches, training leaders, and then moving on. He doesn't operate with an out-of-sight-out-of-mind mentality, but corresponds with groups to reinforce the lessons taught, gives written instructions on new problems, and reminds them that he plans

A Pause To Refresh

to return to check on them. In a text message (a handwritten letter) to one group he writes, "Whatever you have learned or received or heard from me, or seen in me—put it into practice" (Philippians 4:9, NIV).

We may have forgotten the importance of one-on-one training beside a journeyman, but God hasn't. We may call for whomever is available, but God calls the prepared to lead. In training? Ask yourself,

Am I just available, in training, or prepared?

SCARS TELL A STORY

Inside my left forearm, the scar running from my wrist to my elbow is a visible reminder of a painful event when my surgeon removed an artery to replace blocked arteries in my heart. Following surgery, the incision was extremely sensitive to the touch and very ugly. It's a reminder of the one on my chest left by the surgeon who opened my chest to remove a ticking time bomb. My main artery was 98 percent blocked, a widow maker.

The further removed I am from the surgery, the less real it seems to me. The scar is barely visible now. Touching it no longer sends a shock up my arm as it once did, although it still tingles when bumped, reminding me of the lifesaving surgery and the importance of taking better care of my health.

All events, whether personal or national, leave scars on our bodies, soul, or our national conscience. During my lifetime, we've experienced World War II, The Korean Conflict, Vietnam, Desert Storm, Iraq, and Afghanistan, and our troops remain in harm's way. Every war leaves scars on the landscape, participants, and families. The cycle of war seems to be like the tide crashing on the beach with regularity, yet it takes us by surprise.

A heart problem: We want to believe in the inherent goodness of people in spite of ample evidence to the contrary. Jeremiah said: "The human heart is the most deceitful of all things, and desperately wicked. Who really knows how bad it is?" (Jeremiah 17:9). The evil in the heart of the hijackers, not our behavior, drove them to attack us on September 11, 2001. "You want what you don't have, so you scheme and kill to get it. You are jealous of what others have, but you can't get it, so you fight and wage war to take it away from them" (James 4:2). The history of war is the story of tyrants or countries wanting what they don't have—territory, resources, people—and going to war to take it. Ideology may be the spark, but it's ultimately about conquest—they want what someone else has.

A head problem: A two-year-old child puts his little hands over his eyes and pretends we're not there because he can't see us. It's out of sight, out of mind. When bad things happen, our minds want to push them into our subconscious and not remember them. We live in a dangerous and volatile world, as those who hate us are plotting our destruction daily. Behaving like the two-year-old, covering our eyes and pretending they really don't mean us harm doesn't change their minds.

The scar on my left arm is a permanent reminder—life is fragile. Over time, the physical damage of war may be repaired, prompting succeeding generations to forget the horrors of war, so we build war memorials as permanent reminders. Although it's been half a century since our young men fought in the jungles of Vietnam, the scars and stories of that war become very real when we see grown men and hardened warriors weeping as they touch the engraved name of a battle buddy on The Wall.

God instructs Moses to record their first war and reminds them they must never forget the battle. The principle of remembering prompts us to erect the steel and stone memorials to the wars, warriors, and the scars of war. The wounds of life and war leave scars on us personally and on the national psyche. Every scar, like the one on my left arm, tells a story.

What's your story?

LOOK THE OTHER WAY

I stopped by our church to pick up some snack bags we prepared to give to those standing at intersections asking for help. The exit I take off the freeway frequently has someone waiting at the intersection but probably not today; it's cold and raining. Hold that thought...

Many question giving money to a stranger since it might be a scam. That's a good question, but a better question when it's decision time: What did Jesus do?

He is never too busy. We're busy and aren't looking for a stranger in need. In Luke 19: 1-9, Jesus approaches the city of Jericho where a man wants to see Jesus over the crowd; he runs ahead and climbs up in a tree. We don't know if he had a sign, but when Jesus sees him he says, "Zacchaeus! Quick, come down! I must be a guest in your home today." Many grumble; this man is the head IRS guy! Jesus responds, "Salvation has come to this home today, for this man has shown himself to be a true son of Abraham." Zacchaeus is curious to see Jesus, but Jesus sees the need of his soul.

He never looks the other way. When approaching a corner where someone is holding a sign do we stop, avoid eye contact, or look the other way? Jesus is surrounded by throngs pressing up against Him, but when one needy woman touches the hem of His robe, He stops and asks who touched Him. Everyone waits as the woman is brought to Him and he heals her (Matthew 9:20-22).

In response to the question "Who is my neighbor?" Jesus tells a story of a needy Jewish man lying by the roadside (Luke 10:29-37). A priest sees him and goes to the other side of the road; a religious worker stops, takes a look, then he too goes on his way. Finally, a foreigner stops and cares for the man's need, paying cash for his care. The questioner gets the point, and Jesus says, "Now go and do the same."

Should we never look the other way when we see a needy person by the roadside? God is the judge; we need sensitivity to opportunities presented by the roadside. Jesus talks about being cared for when He was hungry, homeless, and sick, in need of clothes, and in prison. The audience racks their brains, can't remember seeing Him in need, then asks Him when they ever did this. He tells them, "When you did it to one of the least of these my brothers and sisters, you were doing it to me!" (Matthew 25:40). He also says to those who look the other way, "When you refused to help the least of these my brothers and sisters, you were refusing to help me" (Matthew 25:45).

The light turns green as I exit the freeway, so I hit the gas thinking I can make the light before it turns red. I'm picking up speed as I turn onto the straightaway, but there he stands! Do I slow down or try to make the light? I slow down; the light changes as I approach. I roll down the window and hand him the bag. He grips my hand; I can't tell if his cheeks were wet from rain or his tears. He crosses the street looking for a place

A Pause To Refresh

out of the rain to eat. As I watch, "Don't forget to show hospitality to strangers, for some who have done this have entertained angels without realizing it!" (Hebrews 13:2) replays in my mind. Was he one of God's angels? If Jesus is standing at the corner, will we stop or

Look the other way?

YOU'LL NEVER WALK ALONE

I was young during WWII and vaguely remember blackouts, ration books, and collecting tin cans to be used for making hypodermic needles. I do remember panic caused by an outbreak of polio. It was believed the virus spread in pools of water, making us fearful of our favorite swimming holes.

The March of Dimes Foundation was established to search for a cure, and their annual fundraising involved passing buckets to collect dimes or other change during intermission at the local theater. Ushers passed popcorn buckets to collect coins, as on the screen, kids with braces on their legs and crutches struggled toward us accompanied by "You'll Never Walk Alone." As the chorus "Walk on through the wind, Walk on through the rain, Though your dreams be tossed and blown. Walk on, walk on, with hope in your heart, And you'll never walk alone, You'll never walk alone" played, coins plunked into the buckets. I'm probably not the only one who wanted to shout, "Keep coming; keep coming. You can make it! You're not alone!"

Dave Carey understands the fear and isolation these kids feel. While flying over Vietnam on August 31, 1967, a missile struck his plane, requiring him to eject. Standing knee deep in a rice paddy, he watched the other planes fly away. One returned and when overhead radioed, "You know we can't come get you." In his book *The Ways We Choose* (Xulon Press, 2014, page 22),

Dave wrote, "I stood out there in the middle of that rice paddy. I felt as though I was the only person in the entire world, out there by myself, alone." Thus began five and one-half years of isolation, brutality, and struggles to maintain hope, unaware that millions were wearing bracelets bearing prisoners' names and praying for their survival and return home.

Step back and join the men and women following Jesus during His ministry. The early enthusiasm becomes confrontational as authorities seek to kill him. Disciples are aware of the atmosphere but gather for Passover dinner with Him (John 13-14). During the course of the evening, He drops a bombshell: "I'm leaving but you're staying here." Imagine the disciples' thoughts: *So this is how it's going to end: We leave everything to follow you, and now we're going to be alone!*

To say it's an interesting evening is an understatement; it generates more questions than answers—an object lesson on foot washing; braggadocio by Peter; conflicting statements: going away but returning, leaving you but you won't be alone, you'll be sad but happy; and a new observance. The most important discussion addresses life without His personal presence and spiritual loneliness. "I will ask the Father, and he will give you another Advocate." (John 14:16).

He:

"will never leave you….leads into all truth" (John 14:16-17) — *Good; he won't leave like Jesus.*

"lives with you now and later will be in you." (John 14:17) — *With us, then in us?*

A Pause To Refresh

is "a gift—peace of mind and heart." (John 14:27) — *Give us some of that!*

Less than twenty-four hours later, Jesus is dead. His disciples are devastated, in hiding until rumors of His resurrection becomes reality. Forty days later, they again enjoy His presence until they receive deployment orders—wait in Jerusalem until the Holy Spirit moves in as promised. "You will receive power when the Holy Spirit comes upon you" (Acts 1:8). Today at the moment of faith, God, in the person of the Holy Spirit, takes up permanent residence (indwelling) in us, and everywhere we go, God goes. Imagine going through a spiritual struggle, and the Holy Spirit whispers in your ear, "Keep going. You can make it." God's Spirit living in us means

We'll never walk alone!

CIRCLE THE WAGONS

A staple plot line of Western movies about settlers heading west in covered wagons involves an attack by a band of either brigands or Indians. When an attack is imminent, the settlers circle the wagons and take up defensive positions using the wagons for cover against the attackers.

Perhaps the script writers were drawing their inspiration from an event from the distant past—or perhaps not. The Israelites were frequently attacked by marauding neighbors and spent many years on a war footing, similar to Israel today. Israel's kings have military advisors, but they also have prophets of God as spiritual advisors (2 Kings 6).

Each time the king of Aram plans a surprise attack against Israel, Elisha the prophet gives the king a heads up so they're prepared. It happens with such frequency the king of Aram demands to know who the traitor is. He is told, "Elisha, the prophet in Israel, tells the king of Israel even the words you speak in the privacy of your bedroom!" (2 Kings 6:12). Elisha is the most wanted man in the region; when the king learns Elisha is in Dothan, he "sent a great army with many chariots and horses to surround the city" (2 Kings 6:14).

Elisha's servant arises early, sees the army and is terrified. He cries, "What will we do now?" and is told "Don't be afraid!...For there are more on our side than on theirs!" The servant might be thinking Elisha is seeing something different,

A Pause To Refresh

but before expressing it, Elisha prays, "Oh Lord, open his eyes and let him see!" When he looks up he sees "the hillside around Elisha was filled with horses and chariots of fire" (2 Kings 6:15-17). Long story short: Elisha is protected, Israel's army is spared, and a feast is held to celebrate the victory before sending the defeated army back to the king of Aram. Take that!

Nice story, you might say, but you expect me to believe God is interested and capable of protecting ME? Yes, but don't take my word for it; allow a group of Marines from 1st Battalion, 5th Marines to share their experience when surrounded and under intense enemy fire. In *A Table in The Presence*, Chaplain Carey Cash shares what his Marines experienced in April 2003 in Baghdad.

An RPG was pointed at one Marine from twenty feet away. As the Marine turned to start shooting, "the man stood up as if he'd seen a ghost...and ran away" (Cash, page 207). An RPG (rocket-propelled grenade) was coming at another so fast he had no opportunity to even close his eyes. "When it was only a few feet away it suddenly jerked up and to the left. As if it were pulled by an unseen rope" (Cash, page 203).

During the worst of the fighting, another "remembered looking at an overpass...and saw that it was lined with AAVs (amphibious assault vehicles) from end to end, like a steel wall... their position on the bridge provided a perfect shield from the incoming rounds that were raining down on us from surrounding rooftops and balconies." Later he searched for the overpass but search as he might "the overpass simply wasn't there" (page 214). Elisha's chariots of fire became American AAVs to protect the Marines!

A Pause To Refresh

God Who surrounds Elisha with His horses and chariots of fire and Who forms a barrier of AAVs to protect Chaplain Cash's Marines in Baghdad from enemy RPGs and hostile fire is capable of protecting us. God *is* our shield of faith "to stop the fiery arrows of the devil" (Ephesians 6:16).

When trouble comes, ask God to open your eyes to see His horses and chariots of fire as He

Circles His wagons!

THE PATCH

At the airport as a soldier walked past, I asked, "How is Chaplain Neuman?" Startled, the young soldier gives me the "How do you know?" look. I pointed to the patch on his shoulder that identified his unit, and we chatted briefly before he headed out to meet family.

Our Army and Marine Corps men and women wear two identifying patches on their shoulders; the unit patch on the left shoulder identifies their unit and a small flag patch on their right shoulder distinguishes them from soldiers of other nations. One of the first official acts when deployed is to uncase and post their unit flag, signaling "this is our territory."

Unit patches or flags have long histories. The Israelites flee Egypt and soon Moses is given organizational instructions. "When the Israelites set up camp, each tribe will be assigned its own area. The tribal divisions will camp beneath their family banners on all four sides of the Tabernacle." When they break camp and move out, "each clan and family set up camp and marched under their banners exactly as the Lord had instructed them" (Numbers 2:2, 34).

In the middle of the night Pharaoh shouts, "Get Out" (Exodus 12:31). He tells them to take their people and stuff and leave (Exodus 12:31-37). Later, cooler heads prevail, asking

"What have we done, letting all those Israelite slaves get away?" Pharaoh's army pursues the fleeing slaves, and Israel is cornered with an army bearing down on them and their backs to the sea. "Didn't we tell you this would happen while we were still in Egypt?" they complain. Moses says "The LORD himself will fight for you. Just stay calm" (Exodus 14:5-14). They do, and God does.

Dust clouds in the distance alert Israel to an approaching army; it's not a regional Welcome Wagon coming for afternoon tea. They're facing war but don't have an army, so what now, Moses? Joshua has twenty-four hours to draft, train, and deploy former slaves to fight a trained army! Great plan, Moses. What can possibly go wrong? The battle goes back and forth, but as Moses's arms are held up by Aaron and Hur, Israel defeats a superior force. The After-Action Report is written, then "Moses built an altar there and named it Yahweh-Nissi (which means 'the LORD is my banner'" (Exodus 17:8-15). Two battles, two different plans—same score: God 2, enemies 0. And three transferrable truths.

God helps us when we're helpless. The saying "God helps those who help themselves" is false! Our efforts to help God leave us as helpless as Moses's mob when they were between the devil (Egyptians) and the deep Red Sea. We can't help ourselves, but "when we were utterly helpless, Christ came...and died for us sinners" (Romans 5:6). Our solution is the same as the Israelites—call on God to help us (Exodus 14:10).

God is our partner in spiritual battles. We're partners with God (2 Corinthians 6:1) with responsibilities to each other.

A Pause To Refresh

"The first time I was brought before the judge…everyone abandoned me.…But the Lord stood with me and gave me strength" (2 Timothy 4:16-17). God has our back!

God places His Yahweh-Nissi patch on us. God identifies us. "By his Spirit he has stamped us with his eternal pledge" (2 Corinthians 1:22, MSG). His invisible patch. Others can identify us as I did the young soldier in the airport: "Your love for one another will prove to the world that you are my disciples" (John 13:35).

The soldier wears his patch with pride and honors its heritage; God expects us to honor

His patch.

A BLACKSMITH SHOP AND FAITH

Mr. Bracken's blacksmith shop was a fun place to visit. I watched as he put dull plow points in his forge and pumped the bellows as cinders and smoke rose above it. When the iron was red hot, he took it out, watched the glowing metal until it reached the right color, dipped it quickly into a tank of water, laid it on his anvil, and skillfully hammered the leading edge, making it sharp again. Before visiting the shop with my dad, I thought dull plow points were sharpened just by visiting his shop.

If the plow points could talk, what would they say about their trip to the blacksmith? You're kidding, right? Nope! God used a talking donkey to speak to Balaam (Numbers 22:28). Let's see the connection between plow points and faith. Visiting the blacksmith shop won't sharpen plow points any more than visiting our holy huddle at church will sharpen faith that's been dulled in the marketplace of daily life.

God is aware. He doesn't watch the evening news and say, "I never thought they would do that." Jesus told His followers: "Here on earth you will have many trials and sorrows" (John 16:33) and "you will be handed over to the courts and will be flogged with whips in the synagogues. You will stand trial before governors and kings because you are my followers" (Matthew 10:16-18). No one could say they didn't know. It's clear faith isn't lived out in God's Witness Protection Program but in a messy world dulling the edge of our spiritual life. When our faith loses its edge, God the Master Smith invites us into His shop.

God is available. When difficulties or setbacks come, what's our first response? A recurring Biblical theme has to do with our attitude toward problems. James says, "When troubles of any kind come your way, consider it an opportunity for great joy" (James 1:2). Peter tells us, "There is wonderful joy ahead, even though you must endure many trials for a little while" (1 Peter 1:6). Paul adds, "We can rejoice, too, when we run into problems and trials" (Romans 5:3). Why should we be happy when troubles come?

God shows up when we have problems and calls for attitude adjustment: "But take heart, because I have overcome the world" (John 16:33) and "God will give you the right words" (Matthew 10:19). Isaiah adds: "Don't be afraid, for I am with you. Don't be discouraged, for I am your God. I will strengthen you and help you. I will hold you up with my victorious right hand" (Isaiah 41:10). His power trumps problems.

God has a purpose. When life hands you lemons, make lemonade. When troubles come, we can blame or look for His purpose. "For you know that when your faith is tested, your endurance has a chance to grow" (James 1:3); "endurance develops strength of character, and character strengthens our confident hope of salvation" (Romans 5:4). Look beyond the problem to the end result. "It is being tested as fire tests and purifies gold—though your faith is far more precious than mere gold" (1 Peter 1:7). How does this work?

A Pause To Refresh

Think plow points, blacksmith, heat, hammer, and God. Just as the plow points were made sharp again in the hands of Mr. Bracken, imagine yourself in the hands of God, the Master Smith of the universe. When trials come, He invites us into His shop, removes us from the heat at the right time, places us on His anvil, and uses the hammer lovingly to

Restore the sharp edge of faith.

IF IT WERE EASY

On July 20, 1969, I sat in my car at Big Sur Campground in California, listening to the radio like other campers. Finally, after a few anxious moments that felt like hours, a voice from 240,000 miles in space crackled. The *Eagle* had landed! We had men on the moon! Everyone in Mission Control and throughout the country breathed a sigh of relief; only later did we learn the lander averted disaster, touching down with only a few seconds of fuel remaining.

Space and computer technology was in its infancy in 1961 when Alan Shepherd was our first to blast into space. John Glenn orbited the earth on February 20, 1962, five years after Russia's *Sputnik*. In the fall of 1962 at Rice University, President John F. Kennedy said:

> We choose to go to the moon in this decade and do the other things, not because they are easy, but because they are hard, because that goal will serve to organize and measure the best of our energies and skills, because that challenge is one that we are willing to accept, one we are unwilling to postpone, and one which we intend to win.

It may not sound like much of a challenge to a generation that has sent spacecraft to Mars and beyond or the discovery of distant galaxies in God's universe with the Hubble Space

A Pause To Refresh

Telescope peering into the night sky. We accepted the challenge, committing manpower, money, and material to the task. In spite of obstacles, setbacks, disappointments, and tragedies, in eight years *Eagle* landed on the moon: mission accomplished. We learned impossible tasks can be done when we're united, organized, and committed to the mission. Hold that thought.

Step back in time to consider a challenge that makes going to the moon seem simple. Jesus challenges His followers to "go and make disciples of all the nations" (Matthew 28:19). "You will be...telling people about me...to the ends of the earth" (Acts 1:8). This challenge is issued to a group of men who likely haven't traveled beyond the boundaries of Israel; going to the ends of the earth is the equivalent of going to the moon—an impossible task.

Challenges, like going to the moon and back, require top talent. We recruit the best and brightest to tackle space, but when recruiting to go to all nations to make disciples, Jesus thinks outside the box. He doesn't pick the educated and cultured or graduates of top seminaries. Instead, He hires rough, uneducated men, fishermen, a tax collector—ordinary men who might fail a background check today.

Roughly ninety percent of new ventures fail in the first three years, and at the end of three years, Jesus's *business* appears to fail. He's dead, and the handpicked successors are in hiding. Following Easter, Jesus's followers undergo continuing education. Training complete, He announces to His trainees the torch is being passed to them. Would a venture capitalist or Wall Street invest in this startup?

A Pause To Refresh

Given their history, it seems His disciple-making venture will fail but something happens. God's Spirit comes upon them as promised, empowering Peter to launch the disciple-making venture with a powerful message. In business terms, sales went through the roof when three thousand respond, showing "all things are possible with God" (Mark 10:27, NIV). Disciple making begins its uninterrupted run.

The torch—make disciples of all the nations—passes to each generation and is in our hands. Nothing changes—the message is the same. It's not easy, we're ordinary people, but His Spirit empowers us. Will we accept the challenge?

It's not easy, but it's doable!

IMPOSSIBLE

In *Christmas Story*, Ralphie wants the holy grail of gifts—The Red Ryder Range Model 200 shot air rifle. The movie revolves around his quest for the air rifle even though everyone, including Santa, says, "You'll shoot your eye out, kid!" Christmas morning anticipation is high as they're opening presents; all the presents are opened, and Ralphie sits on the couch with new clothes but no air rifle.

We're all Ralphie. If we browse our memory banks, we'll find similar experiences—longing for something, only to be disappointed when we finally realize it's not likely to happen. Think of the couple who long to have children; years pass, but the only baby clothes they purchase are for friends. Frustration builds, and medical tests are done until they realize a trip to the maternity ward may never happen; disappointment crushes their spirit.

Disappointment is part of being human, and the most crushing example occurs in and around Jerusalem. Prophets have predicted a coming kingdom for centuries, and now it appears the long-promised Messiah is walking among them as a small band of men join Jesus in training for Kingdom work. Everywhere they go, large crowds come to see Him touching the sick, healing them, showing them the Father, and making disciples. On their last trip to Jerusalem; disciples sense the promised kingdom will be realized as they argue among themselves "about which of them was the greatest" (Luke 9:46). They're mentally picking out their offices, measuring for carpet and drapes. A disappointment lies ahead!

It's Passover, the city is packed with pilgrims, and expectations are off the charts as they enter the city to a welcome rivaling a presidential inaugural parade. Palm branches and garments line the roadway, and His four-legged limo carries Him past as crowds shout, "Hail to the King of Israel!" (John 12:13). Disciples can feel it; they're about to head a new order in the land. By midweek the mood turns ugly; by Friday their hopes are nailed to a cross, the king is dead, and would-be leaders of the new kingdom are in hiding. Two travelers leaving Jerusalem express the prevailing mood of the people: "We had hoped he was the Messiah who had come to rescue Israel" (Luke 24:21). Disappointment turns to despair.

It's always darkest just before dawn. Anyone who has worked a graveyard shift can tell you it seems that the hours before light begins to drive away darkness will never end. Imagine Ralphie sitting on the couch thinking *maybe next year* when his dad points to a package he hadn't seen. Wow. Can it be? Yes, it's the air rifle! Now he can defend his family against Black Bart and his band of bad guys. Disappointment turns to joy.

God makes a way when there is no way. It's early Sunday morning; the wannabe kingdom leaders have slept little since Friday, huddling behind locked doors in fear, grief, and despair. How could they have been so wrong? What did they miss? Under the cover of darkness, some women make their way to the garden tomb to complete proper burial rituals. They have a practical question. "Who will roll away the stone for us from the entrance to the tomb?" (Mark 16:3). They arrive; the stone has been moved. They rush inside; Jesus isn't there. The angel says, "He isn't here! He is risen from the dead" (Mark 16:6). The empty tomb changes everything for them and us!

Years ago, I stood in the tomb the women found empty that morning. I stood there trying to imagine the emotions the women feel as they learn

With God nothing is impossible!

AGAINST ALL ODDS

"They're in front of us, behind us, and we're flanked on both sides by an enemy that outnumbers us 29:1. They can't get away from us now!" So said General Lewis "Chesty" Puller when his Marines were surrounded at the Chosin Reservoir in 1950.

Vegas bookmakers might say of General Puller: He's brave, very brave, but very stupid because the odds against him and his Marines were overwhelming. The odds meant nothing to General Puller; he believed his Devil Dogs could beat any odds. The Marines took heavy casualties but inflicted enormous casualties on the enemy while breaking through the lines. Vegas bookies probably wouldn't bet on the Marines, but they aren't always right. Occasionally someone will bet against the odds and win big.

Imagine a football field with 450 players and 400 cheerleaders on one sideline and one player on the other. The stadium is packed with people, the atmosphere like our Super Bowl. In the middle of the field is the trophy—a wooden altar prepared for sacrifice. The winner will be the gods or God who rains down fire to consume the altar. It's game on. With odds so one-sided, who in their right mind will bet on the one player?

The one player calls out the 450, and in an act of confidence or hubris lets them go first. As the game goes on, they try everything, but when nothing works, Elijah begins talking some smack.

"You'll have to shout louder, for surely he is a god! Perhaps he is daydreaming, or is relieving himself. Or maybe he is away on a trip, or is asleep and needs to be wakened!" (1 Kings 18:27).

Finally, when they're exhausted, Elijah takes the field, and a hush falls on the stands as he increases the odds against success by drenching the altar in water three times. Everyone is on the edge of their seats as he lifts his voice to God. As he starts to pray, you can imagine some snickering among the crowd until the fire of the LORD flashes down from heaven and burns up the young bull, the wood, the stones, and the dust. It even licks up all the water in the trench! And when all the people see it, they fall face down on the ground and cry out, "The LORD—he is God! Yes, the LORD is God!" (1 Kings 18:39).

To recognize the good guys and bad guys, we'll name names. Elijah is on the sideline with only God; the other sideline has 450 priests of false gods and a cheering section of 400 priests of Ashera. The sports-page story is told in 1 Kings 18.

In our increasingly secular world, do you ever get the feeling we're standing alone against all odds? The record of Elijah's validation by God is an example of what Paul meant when he said, "If God is for us, who can be against us?" (Romans 8:31).

Wrong question. "Is God on our side?" Right question: "Are we on God's side?" America was founded by people who believed that God was their rock of safety. Ronald Reagan said,

"I recognize we must be cautious in claiming that God is on our side, but I think it's all right to keep asking if we're on His side." When God is standing on our sideline and the odds are 850 to 1 against us, ignore the Vegas bookies because:

If God is against us, it doesn't matter who is for us!

If God is for us, it doesn't matter who is against us!

WAITING, AND WAITING, AND WAITING AND...

The light turned red just as I arrived at the intersection; even though I was heading to an important meeting, the light wasn't impressed. Waiting for the light to change, I was stewing and about as patient as a child waiting for Christmas. The light kept me waiting forever, but as I sat, I began to wonder: How much of my life is spent waiting for traffic lights to change?

Research suggests we spend thirty-eight hours per year waiting in traffic. Assuming a normal life expectancy, that's about one year of our life spent sitting still in traffic. Road rage explained. Add the time waiting at the store, the doctor's office, and airport security, as well as for our spouse to get ready to go, and it's a miracle we get anything done. We can't avoid waiting, but can we avoid wasting time while waiting?

Time isn't partial. I was extremely busy doing God's work and thought it would be nice if He would take a few hours a day from someone who was wasting them and give them to me. I could get more done, but that would be playing favorites, and "God does not show favoritism" (Romans 2:11).

Don't be paranoid—the light isn't out to get you or me. While waiting, I looked around and saw people sitting in a limo, in an expensive car, and in a clunker. The rich and the day laborer all wait for the light to change. Jesus said God "gives his sunlight to both the evil and the good, and he sends rain on the just and the unjust alike" (Matthew 5:45).

Time is a gift. Each week the TV show "60 Minutes" opens with a stopwatch ticking toward zero—a reminder that birth begins our internal clock's countdown until zero days remain. Time is measured in twenty-four-hour segments and waits for no one. Game clocks in stadiums let everyone know when the game is winding down, but only God knows when our time will expire. A line in many obituaries—"He died unexpectedly"—is a reminder we're not in control. "LORD, remind me how brief my time on earth will be…that my days are numbered—how fleeting my life is" (Psalm 39:4).

Time is a stewardship. The allowance is a tool to teach children how to handle money. Both money and time are resources; stewardship of time is as critical, if not more so, as stewardship of money. ARRRRGH, the light was still red. How can we make time stewardship rather than stewing?

Pray without ceasing (1 Thessalonians 5:17, MSG). It's a good use of time while waiting, but keep your eyes open. The light will change, and you'll hear horns. Waiting in line is a chance to look for opportunities to redeem the time (Ephesians 5:15) with a smile or kind word. Seldom do we go to doctor appointments that don't involve waiting. We can read three-year-old news magazines, look at other patients, use our phone device, or bring something to do. I always carry a binder with different things to work on, and it seems the wait is never long when I'm busy.

A Pause To Refresh

We can control how we wait, but not where or how long we wait. In 2006 when we were packing boxes for our chaplains, Gary Campbell and I would take the boxes to the Post Office. We always seemed to arrive at the busiest time of day, but Gary had a plan. I waited in line with the wagon, while Gary redeemed the time by going down the line telling each person about Adopt-a-Chaplain and giving them a brochure.

Wait we will, but how we wait is up to us.

GOD WILL GET YOU

Bea Arthur, a quick-witted, sassy lady, played Maude in the popular sitcom by that name from 1972 to 1979. Walter, not the sharpest knife in the drawer, was a perfect foil for Maude's barbs. Occasionally when he did something to exasperate her, she would raise one eyebrow, give him that look all men know, and say, "God will get you for that!" We laughed, but her statement feeds the perception of God as an angry enforcer waiting to get us. Was Maude right about God?

God is angry. Ah-ha! Maude was right. God stands ready to get us the minute we step out of line! Paul says, "The wrath of God is being revealed from heaven against all the godlessness and wickedness of people" (Romans 1:18, NIV), followed by a long list of bad behavior until God "abandoned them to their foolish thinking" (Romans 1:18). When pushed to His limit, God doesn't *get them*—He leaves them to their own devices.

God's anger is directed at the acts, not the actors; against the sin, not the sinner! An angry owner may say, "Bad dog for...," and the poor pup thinks his master is angry at him, not the mess he made. God's anger is aimed at the wrong, not the person.

God is love. God's love doesn't let us off the hook; we're accountable for what we do. We say, "Love is blind," but God's love is neither blind nor passive; it's proactive: "God demonstrates his own love for us in this: While we were still sinners, Christ died for us" (Romans 5:8, NIV). For the person from Missouri, God doesn't just say "I love you," He directs His love toward our need.

Children are an occupational hazard of parenthood, or as one author observed, "Children don't make good pets." The best illustration of the depth of God's love is the steadfast and almost fanatical love of a mother for her children, even when they push limits and continually step over her lines in the sand. "If it weren't my child I'd disown him/her" has probably crossed the mind of many moms, but very few actually do. Dad's fuse is much shorter.

Anger…Love are two strong emotions as incompatible as oil and water. We can't bring the two together, but God does by His grace. Grace is more than a blue-eyed blonde; it's a (χαρις) gift. "God saved you by his grace…it is a gift from God" (Ephesians 2:8). Two important concepts: it's free, and it requires a response. God offers freedom from His anger at our sin, but we must accept it.

I was a good citizen in high school, but once when I was called to the principal's office, he told me to bring my books as I was suspended for three days. I slowly walked to my locker; facing the principal or police was preferable to facing my dad if I had misbehaved. I knew he loved me but would be angry. I returned to the office and put my books on the principal's desk. As I was leaving, he asked, "If I let you stay in school, will you behave?" "Yes!" I accepted his (χαρις) offer, my infraction was forgiven, and he never mentioned it again.

A Pause To Refresh

Grace is how God removes the barricade between His anger and His love. Maude was wrong—God's not out to get us; instead He offers the gift of forgiveness through His grace. John Newton captured God's heart with: "Amazing grace! how sweet the sound, that saved a wretch like me; I once was lost but now am found, was blind but now I see." Receive his gift and experience His

Amazing grace!

SECURE...INSECURE

Our squadron deployed one month prior to the end of my enlistment, but the needs of the service required a ninety-day extension. I had to sign it, or I would have been kept until the carrier returned in nine months. I signed the extension, we deployed, the ninety days passed. I left the carrier off the coast of Japan and arrived at Treasure Island Naval Base three days before the ninety-day extension expired. Small problem: 1000 sailors were waiting, and they processed only 100 per day. I had to wait my turn!

Over the next ten days, *The San Francisco Chronicle* printed two special editions daily. Really big headlines suggested war was imminent, adding to my anxiety and fear the Navy would say, "You're going back to the carrier." The hot spot: The Middle East; the year: 1958! Since then, the region has been ground zero of constant tensions. The attack on 9/11 shattered our sense of security and made it our priority. Can we ever feel secure again? Yes, but first we must recognize some basics.

Internal Security. It's been said if you can keep calm with all that's swirling around us, you just don't know what is going on. Government can't provide security; God's promise doesn't guarantee physical safety, but it does give us what we need. During the last dinner with His disciples, Jesus walks them through things that trouble them. Toward the end, he says, "I am leaving you with a gift—peace of mind and heart. And the peace I give is a gift the world cannot give. So don't be troubled or afraid" (John 14:27). Only God can provide internal security.

External Security. Government's first responsibility is to keep our homeland safe, but increasing acts of terrorism worldwide super-size our insecurities. Egypt, Babylon, Greece, and Rome all fell, not because their armies were weak, but because of an attitude described by Isaiah: "What sorrow awaits those… trusting their horses, chariots, and charioteers and depending on the strength of human armies instead of looking to the Lord" (Isaiah 31:1). Our security isn't in tanks, Congress, the FDIC, locked doors, or loaded .44 Magnums, but in God.

Eternal Security. Millions carry passports from the country of their birth but choose to immigrate to our country and become citizens of two countries. When addressing the struggles of daily life, Paul reminds us of our dual citizenship: "But we are citizens of heaven, where the Lord Jesus Christ lives" (Philippians 3:20). We're citizens of earth by someone else's choice but citizens of heaven by our choice, an act of faith.

Our eternal security is more valuable than any security government might provide. A friend put it in perspective when he said, "You're not going to get off this earth alive." Jesus said, "Don't be afraid of those who want to kill your body; they cannot touch your soul" (Matthew 10:28). Christians from Egypt modeled this as the terrorists prepared to behead them. The Christians didn't plead—they prayed, secure in their heavenly citizenship. Jesus talks with His disciples about the insecurity they'll face, then says, "But take heart, because I have overcome the world" (John 16:33).

A Pause To Refresh

My first semester at Dallas Seminary, Dr. Toussaint began every class session with our singing, "More secure is no one ever, than the loved ones of the Savior—Not yon star on high abiding, nor the bird in home nest hiding." He drilled into our heads and hearts the security we have in God. If I weren't absolutely sure God is in control, I'd be a basket case. It's not about who wins a battle but who wins the war! When insecurities come,

Relax—God has this!

IT'S NOT COMPLICATED

Humans have perfected the ability to take the simple and make it incomprehensible. Congress may pass a law that makes sense, but the professional bureaucrats bury simplicity under reams of paper, requiring a lawyer and an accountant to comply. President Reagan said, "Government is inherently incompetent, and no matter what task it is assigned, it will do it in the most expensive and inefficient way possible." It's human nature.

The Ten Commandments (Exodus 20) outline the code of conduct God expects of His people. "You shall have no other gods before me" means idols, wealth, family, or anything else must not be more important than our relationship with God. Similar clarifications for the other nine, as well as offerings to restore our relationship when we fail, are given through Moses.

From simple to complex. Once God's law is in stone, religious bureaucrats, presuming to speak for God, take over, replacing the simplicity of the law with reams of rules and traditions necessary to keep the law. "Remember the Sabbath to keep it holy" generated hundreds of specific rules detailing what is and is not permitted (how far you can walk, what you can carry, food preparation, washing of hands) required to keep the Sabbath holy. *Fiddler on the Roof* opens with Tevye talking about their rules and traditions and concludes with "Because of our traditions, everyone knows who he is and what God expects him to do."

Unfortunately, that mentality creeps into the church as some self-appointed religious inspectors define what is and is not appropriate behavior for Jesus followers. It may be subtle or direct rules good Christians observe. Years ago, a pastor was listing the dos and don'ts his church had for teens. After listening to his list, my comment was, "That's legalism, and it's wrong." His reply: "Yes, but it works!" Does it? Think about that.

From Complex to Simple. Frequent verbal jousts occur between Jesus and the religious bureaucrats. He's criticized for not following the ritual handwashing before meals. It gets testy until He says, "What sorrow also awaits you experts in religious law! For you crush people with unbearable religious demands, and you never lift a finger to ease the burden" (Luke 11:46). As He's "leaving, the teachers of religious law…tried to provoke him with many questions…to trap him into saying something they could use against him" (Luke 11:53-54). They never learned but kept trying.

A religious expert asks, "Which is the most important commandment?" It's not complicated: "Love the Lord your God with all your heart, all your soul, and all your mind…Love your neighbor as yourself. The entire law and all the demands of the prophets are based on these two commandments (Matthew 22:36-40). It's simple: Love God; love your neighbor.

The pastor was comfortable saying their rules work with teens in the church. I responded, "They may appear to work while they're still teens, but will the rules work when the teens become adults?" Experience says no! Why not keep it simple as Jesus did? "Love…God…Love your neighbor."

A commercial by the USPS is a practical illustration. In a conversation with a letter carrier, the businessman says, "I sell tools because tools aren't complicated. Know what's complicated? Shipping." The carrier replies, "Not really. With flat rate boxes, shipping is easy. If it fits, it ships." The owner says, "That's not complicated!"

We frequently hear, "What would Jesus do?" His encounter with the religious experts concerning the rules for Christ followers is this:

It's simple; don't complicate it.

GOING IN CIRCLES

A group of scouts on a night hike were to follow the river north about three miles, then cut across the woods to the designated camping area. The team leader looked at a map, saw that about halfway to their destination, the river made a big horseshoe loop and turned back about a quarter mile straight ahead. When they arrived at the location during a rest break, they decided to take a shortcut across the narrow distance rather than follow the map.

About an hour later when it started raining hard, they erected the pup tent designed for two, and seven boys jammed into it trying to keep dry. The rain subsided; they emerged from the tent soaking wet and saw the wrapper of a candy bar one of them ate during the rest stop! They'd walked in circles for an hour and were back where they decided to ignore the map.

The voice of reason. The boys decided taking a shortcut made sense, but their decision didn't end well. Israel departs Egypt on a camping trip; the Promised Land is just ahead. Twelve men investigate the land and give a Billy Goat report: the land is great, but it's hard! The majority would rather return to slavery, and a ten-day trip stretches into forty years of going in circles until all the adults who objected to the shortcut died. The lesson: "There is a way that appears to be right but in the end it leads to death" (Proverbs 14:12, NIV). I wonder how many times they circled back to the spot the decision was made to take the long away around rather than God's way and thought, "This place looks familiar"?

The voice of God. We know God audibly spoke to Moses from the burning bush, but how do we react when someone says, "God told me to…?" Some may dismiss statements like that, but God speaks to us. "Although the Lord gives you the bread of adversity and the water of affliction, your teachers will be hidden no more; with your own eyes you will see them. Whether you turn to the right or to the left, your ears will hear a voice behind you, saying, 'This is the way; walk in it'" (Isaiah 30:20-21, NIV).

God speaks to us through Jesus's words and life. "Long ago God spoke many times and in many ways to our ancestors through the prophets. And now in these final days, he has spoken to us through his Son" (Hebrews 1:1-2).

Jesus and the prophets are no longer present, but Jesus promised we would not be without a voice via the spiritual gifts given to the church. "To one there is given through the Spirit a message of wisdom, to another a message of knowledge by means of the same Spirit" (1 Corinthians 12:8, NIV). When unsure, seek counsel from others who understand how God's wisdom can be applied to a given situation.

The choice. It's not enough to hear, "This is the way; walk in it." A choice is required, and all choices have consequences. The scouts had a map with clear directions but decided they had a better way; they got lost, walked in circles, got soaked, and spent the night in the woods rather than in camp. Israel on a camping trip chooses to reject God's roadmap and learn their choice "leads to death" when all adults who rejected God's voice miss their destiny and spend the rest of their lives wandering in circles in the desert.

Do you ever feel like you've lost your way and are going in circles? Listen for God's quiet voice:

"This is the way; walk in it."

A FEW GOOD MEN

"God doesn't need an army to guarantee a win; He just needs a few good men." Pentagon planners aren't likely to be impressed by the advice in the song "A Few Good Men" by the Gaither Vocal Band. War is brutal, mistakes are unforgiving, and every commander knows the best battle plan becomes obsolete after the first shot is fired, but odds of success improve when you have superior numbers and firepower.

A crowd of wannabe disciples is following Jesus when He says, "Don't begin until you count the cost." At that moment, perhaps a cohort of Roman soldiers is passing by, providing a good illustration as he asks, "What king would go to war against another king without first sitting down with his counselors to discuss whether his army of 10,000 could defeat the 20,000 soldiers marching against him?" (Luke 14:28-33). The point: If you're outnumbered, it's time to rethink your strategy.

An Army of One. When the Philistines are in a foul mood they take it out on their Hebrew neighbors. Armies line up opposite each other for combat (1 Samuel 17) but with a new wrinkle, a *mano-a-mano* fight between one soldier from each side while everyone cheers for their guy. Sounds reasonable until the Philistine, who is over nine feet tall, steps forth, walking back and forth, talking smack for forty days unchallenged until David, a visiting teenager, accepts the challenge. Everyone believes the big guy is the prohibitive favorite.

Stepping onto the battlefield, the teen says, "Everyone assembled here will know that the LORD rescues his people, but not with sword and spear. This is the LORD's battle, and he will give you to us!" (1 Samuel 17:47). Final score: David 1, Goliath 0!

A Few Good Men. The Midianites are making life unbearable for the Hebrews until God chooses Gideon to deliver payback (Judges 6). His call for volunteers brings thirty-two thousand men ready for war. As they prepare for battle, God says to Gideon, "You have too many warriors with you. If I let all of you fight the Midianites, the Israelites will boast to me that they saved themselves by their own strength" (Judges 7:2). The enemies are like swarms of locusts and thirty-two thousand are too many? You're kidding, right? No, Gideon has an army of 30,000 when he needs only a few good men.

Force reduction: If afraid, go home. Twenty-two thousand leave. Lapping water like a dog eliminates nine thousand seven hundred, leaving only three hundred, less than one percent for what's likely a suicide mission. A recon mission complete, three groups of one hundred head out, each armed with a sword, a trumpet, a torch, and jar to cover the torch. Gideon signals; they blow their trumpets, breaking the pitchers and revealing the torches, and shout, "A sword for the Lord and for Gideon!" (Judges 7:18). The Midianites, confused and terrified, turn on each other. With God's help and three hundred men, the Midianites are routed by a few good men.

A lesson for today. Do you ever wake up facing problems like swarms of locusts and feel you're outnumbered and outgunned? Paul writes about our relationship with God and asks the question, "With God on our side...how can we lose?" (Romans 8:31, MSG). The answer is we can't! But if God is against us, we can't win.

President Reagan said, "We must be cautious in claiming that God is on our side, but I think it's all right to keep asking if we're on His side." God doesn't need an army to win; He needs only

A few good men and women!

SEARCHING

"Gonna find her, Gonna find her." The opening line of a song by The Coasters reinforced the writer's determination to find his love, wherever she may be. He enlists well-known detectives of the era—Sam Spade, Sergeant Friday, Boston Blackie, Bulldog Drummond, and Charlie Chan. The song topped the R&B charts for twelve weeks in 1957. Google the song "Searchin'." Listen to it; feel pain, emptiness in the rhythm and words. We then realize…

We're still "searchin every which a-way." I Googled "searching for love" and 296,000,000 items popped up in less than a second. Wow! It's more widespread than I thought. Scanning a few pages suggested each writer has a different secret for finding love, but broaden the search to include purpose and meaning and the suggestions are infinite. We want an easy solution, but…

We're searching in all the wrong places. Our search is for something to fulfill our emptiness. Common threads of advice in our search for love, purpose, and meaning include a new job, house, or spouse. We make the changes, but we're still searching, knowing there's more to life than just living it. Our emptiness is internal, not external.

We're all searching for that one thing. In the film *City Slickers,* Mitch asked Curley, the crusty old cowboy, "What's the meaning of life?" Curley held up one finger and said it's about finding one thing. Jesus tells us He came to bring that one thing: "A rich and satisfying life" (John 10:10). That's the essence of our search. It's available, but where is it?

God's answer is as plain as the nose on our face. Paul says creation posts road signs pointing us to God: "Through everything God made, they can clearly see his invisible qualities—his eternal power and divine nature," but we have a better idea and our "minds became dark and confused" (Romans 1:20-21), and we look elsewhere.

God allows us to go our own way, yet His divine magnetic north remains embedded in us. Augustine's search for fulfillment leaves him so weary he cries out, "O Lord, how long? how long, Lord?" He finds forgiveness of sin and starts a journey of discovery. He marvels at the greatness, power, and wisdom of God and by comparison our insignificance, yet to God, we're more than a lump of clay. He writes, "You have made us for yourself, and our hearts are restless, until they can find rest in you." Our search for fulfillment begins and ends with God.

We were at a party for my oldest grandson's second birthday. When the time came to open his presents, we all watched as he ripped the paper off each package and looked at it briefly before grabbing the next one. About halfway through the pile, he ripped open a package, looked at it, then went into the other room to play with it. He found what he wanted, so he quit looking. His uncle knew little boys are looking for toys, not clothes. God knows and provides what we're seeking.

The ancients' search for meaning gives us direction. Blaise Pascal, a seventeenth-century philosopher, scientist, and author, writes about the search for meaning. His aha moment came when he realized stuff can't fill the void "because the infinite abyss can only be filled by an infinite and immutable object, that is to say, only by God Himself" (Pensées VII, 425).

Augustine, Pascal, The Coasters, and Curly are right. Are you ready to end your search? The Psalmist (Psalm 46:10) says the object of our search is not *something* but *someone*!

"Be still and know that I am God!"

GET ME TO THE CHURCH

People at a church business meeting were discussing how to get those who consistently arrive fifteen minutes late to church on time. They decided to start services fifteen minutes earlier. Start time is immaterial to those who operate on CST (Christian Standard Time): fifteen minutes late. Start time was changed to 10:45, and those on CST did arrive fifteen minutes earlier, at 11:00 instead of 11:15.

We're in our seats before a movie starts; at the scheduled hour, the movie is always preceded by previews of coming attractions. Like the movies, most church services are predictable: music, announcements, offering, and the sermon. One church service broke the pattern by starting the message after two songs. A man operating on CST came in, was surprised, and gave the pastor a "What's up?" look while pointing to his watch. The main event started without him.

Practical Priorities. Our use of time reveals our priorities. My dad's rule: "I'd rather be an hour early than one minute late." Days prior to the release of the latest Apple phone, customers line up, even sleeping on the street for days to be the first to get one. The new phone is temporary while church represents eternity, yet some who arrive early for a phone will be late for church. When was the last time you saw people lined up for a church service?

Practical Consequences. Our time allocation shows what's important to us. While stationed at NAS Moffett Field, four of us started playing pinochle after work every day, rushing back to the barracks and playing until lights out. Nothing was more important to us than cards *except* chow. We knew when the mess hall next door closed and were there before that time! Arrive one minute late and the next chow call was at 0600 hours.

Eternal Consequences. Is God flexible? Jesus uses weddings to illustrate the importance of being on time. He frequently talks about what the Kingdom of Heaven is like but purposely leaves open the *when*, leading to many guesses. In Matthew 25, Jesus focuses on preparation; the chapter begins, "The Kingdom of Heaven will be like ten bridesmaids who took their lamps and went to meet the bridegroom."

The bridegroom doesn't show up until midnight! Five prepare as if the wedding will start on time, five as though it won't. They fall asleep, their lamps run out of oil, at midnight they hear, "Look, the bridegroom is coming! Come out and meet him!" Five go into the wedding; five go to town for oil, but when they get back they're late and miss the wedding. They call "Lord! Lord! Open the door for us!" But he called back, "Believe me, I don't know you!" The point of the story: Be prepared! "So you, too, must keep watch! For you do not know the day or hour of my return" (Matthew 25:1-13).

Consistently arrive for work fifteen minutes late, and you'll have plenty of time to stand in line for the latest phone but no money to buy it. Have you ever gone to a store on the last day of a buy-one-get-one-free sale and arrived after the store was closed? You missed out on a bargain.

A Pause To Refresh

Jesus spoke frequently about His return, prompting questions of when; since then many experts think they've broken God's code on when; people get excited, but 100 percent of the predictions have proven false. Jesus said, "And since you don't know when that time will come, be on guard! Stay alert!" (Mark 13:33). We know Jesus will return but not when; He will be on time, so

Don't be late!

NOT AGAIN

TV talking heads use "Active Shooter" to announce another mass shooting. Before the smoke clears, politicians are on air saying we need more gun laws, but it's not that simple. I grew up in the 1940s and -50s, when everyone had guns. Students came to school with rifles on the gun racks of unlocked trucks, and gun safety was taught in schools. Gun laws were few; there were no background checks or gun registrations. Mass shootings were rare, but no longer.

FBI stats show from 1900 to 1970, we had twenty-eight mass shootings (four per decade); from 1970 to 2015, we had 273 (sixty per decade). The increase in recent decades comes in spite of more laws aimed at restricting gun ownership. Common sense says it's not guns.

If not guns, then what triggered this downward spiral? Jeremiah told Israel turning away from God causes heart disease. "The human heart is the most deceitful of all things, and desperately wicked" (Jeremiah 17:9).

Late in the nineteenth century, Nietzsche advanced a radical idea for his time when he said, "God is dead. God remains dead. And we have killed him." Fortunately, for decades the debate was among philosophers until April 8, 1966, when the cover of *Time* asked, "Is God Dead?" In responding that God is dead, Professor William Hamilton of Colgate Rochester

A Pause To Refresh

Divinity School said openly what he and some radical professors were thinking. The question was in the public domain, openly challenging the beliefs of 93 percent of Americans who believed God was alive and well. Pew research in 2014 showed the number of believers at that time to be 65 percent. To accomplish this drop in four decades, God's opponents mounted a two-pronged attack against Him—educational and legal.

Education. Killing God was a long-range project and required removing Him from the schools. At one time, teachers regularly read the Bible and prayed in class. The Supreme Court ruled in 1964 that teachers could no longer lead prayer or read the Bible, even on a voluntary basis—expelling God from school! Students can be suspended for bringing a Bible on some campuses; Christian after-school clubs are seldom approved. Bibles and prayer are welcome in prisons but not in schools. Is it possible we'd need fewer in prisons if we'd allow prayer and Bibles back in the classroom?

Legal. Efforts to kill God moved to the courts. For more than 200 years, the first amendment to the Constitution, "Congress shall make no law respecting an establishment of religion, or prohibiting the free exercise thereof," guaranteed God a seat at the table of government and in the public square. Courts now rule that God's presence in the public square—whether it is a cross, nativity scene, or monuments to our war dead containing a cross—violates the establishment clause. They haven't tried to remove the crosses from Arlington Cemetery.

Results. Actions have consequences. The Psalmist declares, "Blessed is the nation whose God is the Lord" (Psalm 33:12, NIV); the opposite is also true. Paul writes about the consequences when people kicked God out of their lives: "God gave them over in the lusts of their hearts to impurity... to degrading passions" (Romans 1:24, 26). If God Is dead, we have no moral compass; history is on a continuous loop of "In those days Israel had no king; everyone did as they saw fit" (Judges 21:25, NIV), replayed with each mass shooting.

Remedy. Barbara Brown Taylor asks, "Does God still believe in humans?" Return to God and we'll see the answer is yes. He promises, "if my people, who are called by my name, will humble themselves and pray and seek my face and turn from their wicked ways, then I will hear from heaven, and I will forgive their sin and will heal their land" (2 Chronicles 7:14, NIV).

Jeremiah was right:

We have a heart problem!

THE RIGHT QUESTION

"I feel like my heart has been ripped out and torn into little pieces," an anguished mother cried as we stood by her daughter's bed in ICU. The life support machines were no longer blinking, beeping, or clicking, and the staff stood silently as we felt the anguish of a mother who has just lost her child.

Five days earlier, Toni had major surgery. We were making plans to take her home in a few days, but a terrible hospital mistake changed plans from a homecoming to a vigil by her bedside. Mom's call trumped my plans for the day; I rushed to the hospital to be with my friends. After talking to the doctors, by noon we were coming to grips with the grim reality, so Mom and I spent time walking around the hallways absorbing that reality.

Late in the day, we left ICU and gathered with the family in a conference room for a meeting with hospital staff, but in a few minutes a knock on the door summoned us back to ICU. Toni slipped into eternity, and we weren't there with her.

Scenes like this are played out every day in homes, on the highways, and in hospitals around the country. When it happens, the first question grieving families ask is "Why?" I believe the question crying out this from Mom's heart isn't "Why?" but "God, where were you?" As we thought back over the day, the question answered itself.

God was with us as we walked the hallways. Nurses stopped us to ask, "Are you okay?" That was God. Friends hugged Chris in the hallway with tears in their eyes. That was God. When we were sitting in the cafeteria, a complete stranger walked up and sat down to talk. That was God. They were all His hands and hearts letting us know He was there with us.

God was in the ICU with Toni holding her hand and finally whispering enough, releasing her from all pain, as she reached out and touched His face. We were out of the room, but Toni didn't die alone. God was there with her and understood our pain and questions. He was there two thousand years ago on Good Friday afternoon when Jesus cried, "It is finished!"

God's promise. It's easy to say God is with us when things are going well, but when tragedy visits, it's easier to focus on our problem rather than His promise. God doesn't promise us a rose garden, but He does promise His presence. "For the Lord your God will personally go ahead of you. He will neither fail you nor abandon you" (Deuteronomy 31:6) and "I will never fail you. I will never abandon you" (Hebrews 13:5).

God's presence in times of trouble. Daniel's enemies concoct a scheme to feed him to hungry lions, but the lions lose their appetites. When asked how he survives, Daniel says, "My God sent his angel to shut the lions' mouths so that they would not hurt me" (Daniel 6:22). Another plot to turn three Hebrews into crispy critters fails, and the King says, "I see four men, unbound, walking around in the fire unharmed! And the fourth looks like a god...He sent his angel to rescue his servants who trusted in him" (Daniel 3:25, 28.) Paul, in a Roman prison facing death, says, "Everyone abandoned me....But the Lord stood with me and gave me strength....And he rescued me from certain death" (2 Timothy 4:16-17).

When bad things happen to us most ask the wrong question: Why is this happening to us? The right question: God, where are you? His answer is,

"I am with you always" (Matthew 28:20).

GOING WITH THE FLOW

The Alaskan salmon's journey begins going with the flow from a peaceful river upstream where they hatch, down the rapids from the fresh waters into the salt water and rough surf of the Pacific Ocean. They spend about two years avoiding predators and fishermen until their biological clock and internal GPS directs them on the difficult journey back to where life began.

The journey home, going against the flow, is hard. River currents are strong, rapids they must jump are a challenge, and hungry predators along the way are waiting for a salmon dinner. Most don't have the energy to continue the challenging journey; less than ten percent make it back to the stream of their birth to spawn. If all were to decide the upstream journey is too difficult, wild salmon would become extinct.

The life cycle of wild salmon illustrates our faith—it begins peacefully, but obstacles and challenges increase over time. Jesus gives us a heads up: "In this world you will have trouble" (John 16:33, NIV). We're warned about the identity of our most dangerous predator: "Watch out for your great enemy, the devil. He prowls around like a roaring lion, looking for someone to devour" (1 Peter 5:8). Our faith life turns on two decisions we make.

Going with the flow is easy. The temptation to go along may be over something simple. Peter joins a group of men warming their hands by the fire on a cold evening until a young girl walks by, points at him, and says "You were one of those with Jesus of Nazareth" (Mark 14:67). All eyes are on Peter; what will he do? Jesus is on trial inside, and it can be dangerous to admit he's a follower, so he claims mistaken identity. He's given two more opportunities to acknowledge Jesus before he emphatically says, "A curse on me if I'm lying—I don't know this man you're talking about!" (Mark 14:71). When our faith is challenged, changing the subject might feel right, but is it?

Going against the flow is hard. As the salmon heads upstream, it's hard and most give up. Jesus tells His followers some hard truths. They ask, "How can anyone accept it?" and upon confirmation "many of his disciples turned away and deserted him." They weren't willing to go against the flow (John 6:60, 66). It takes courage to face imprisonment or death to follow Christ. Peter and John are arrested and told to explain themselves. Peter's bold defense of their faith stuns the council, and they "recognized them as men who had been with Jesus" (Acts 4:13).

The history of the church is stained with the blood of many who chose to go against the flow, choosing imprisonment or death, but here at home we've been exempt until now. The same pressure used to silence first-century faith is becoming more open as some citizens face ridicule, fines, and jail for practicing their faith. Television gives us a ringside seat as Christians in other parts of the world are beheaded, shot, stoned, burned, and crucified. Their crime—refusing to deny faith in Christ. In the US, we may never face similar life-or-death situations, but descendants of those who killed early Christians say they're coming for us.

A Pause To Refresh

Troubles will come, and we shouldn't be surprised. Jesus said, "I have told you these things, so that in me you may have peace....But take heart! I have overcome the world" (John 16:33, NIV). How we respond to trouble will tell those around us if our faith is real or not. Will they recognize me as

One who has been with Jesus?

THE BLOOD BANK

Settled science is frequently unsettled by facts. Medical experts once used leeches and bloodletting to treat disease, but we've come a long way in understanding the body God created, particularly the importance of blood to life.

Martin R. DeHaan, M.D., wrote:

> The blood is fluid and mobile, that is, it is not limited to one part of the body but is free to move throughout the entire body and touch every other fixed cell as it supplies it with nourishment and carries off waste products and the ashes of cell activity which we call metabolism.
>
> In the normal human body there are about five pints of this fluid, and this blood pumped by the heart circulates through the system about every twenty-three seconds, so that every cell in the body is constantly supplied and cleansed and at the same time is in constant communication and touch with every other cell in that body.…Once the blood fails to reach the cells and members of the body, they promptly die and no man ever dies until his blood ceases to circulate (https://www.jesus-is-savior.com/BTP/Dr_MR_DeHaan/Chemistry/01.htm).

Physical life is in the blood. Perhaps the phrase most overlooked for centuries is "The life of every creature is in its blood" (Leviticus 17:14). That line of code, when understood, revolutionized medicine, ended bloodletting, and established blood banks to have lifesaving blood available when needed. God's instructions for worship emphasizes the importance of blood.

The more we learn about our bodies the more we appreciate David's words, "Thank you for making me so wonderfully complex! Your workmanship is marvelous—how well I know it" (Psalm 139:14). The importance of blood for physical life illustrates a more profound spiritual truth:

Eternal life is in the blood. Our relationship with God is fractured and we're separated from Him, but He established a way back—blood. Worship instructions draw a parallel between blood and life—both physical and spiritual. "The life of the body is in its blood. I have given you the blood on the altar to purify you, making you right with the LORD. It is the blood, given in exchange for a life, that makes purification possible" (Leviticus 17:11). Passover provides a picture when God says, "When I see the blood, I will pass over you" (Exodus 12:13).

Throughout the Old Testament, the sacrifices are made to cover sins of the people and maintain relationship with God. Over time, however, the sacrifices became a religion instead. Jesus comes to break the ritual and restore our relationship with God. John introduces Jesus and a radical new idea—He's "The Lamb of God who takes away the sin of the world!" (John 1:29). They understand covering sin (atonement), but taking away sin is new and resonates with the people.

A Pause To Refresh

The death and resurrection of Jesus establishes the way back to a relationship with God and is the theme for all mankind—both Jew and Gentile. Paul comes back to the themes "Christ, our Passover Lamb, has been sacrificed for us" (1 Corinthians 5:7) and "Once you were far away from God, but now you have been brought near to him through the blood of Christ" (Ephesians 2:13).

The importance of blood became personal to me during bypass surgery. At one point my heart was stopped for almost two hours while three clogged arteries were replaced. I would have been dead in seconds were it not for the heart/lung bypass machine cleaning and pumping blood through my body until my heart was brought back online. Fortunately, I didn't need a blood transfusion.

God's Blood Bank is open 24/7, and the welcome mat is out; there is no waiting and no shortage; it has your type, and all are welcome. William Cowper put this truth to music in 1772: "There is a fountain filled with blood, Drawn from Immanuel's veins, And sinners plunged beneath that flood, Lose all their guilty stains....Redeeming love has been my theme and shall be till I die." For all you do,

His blood's for you.

STOP, THIEF!

"Space: the final frontier. These are the voyages of the Starship Enterprise. Its five-year mission: to boldly go where no man has gone before." We first heard those words on September 8, 1966. Little did we realize the fictional voyages of the *Enterprise* mirror a real journey of discovery, moving us at warp speed from the Stone Age of communication to the electronic age.

The speed and convenience of electronic communication comes with significant risks. Every time we turn on our electronics, cyberspace trolls are sifting through data, seeking cracks in our security allowing them to steal what is ours—our identity. Target, Sony, or government agencies with large IT departments can't stop hackers, so our chances of being hacked are about 100 percent. Identity theft isn't a product of the electronic age.

Identity theft precedes us. In a galaxy far, far away, Lucifer, a prince among angels, says "I will…be like the Most High" (Isaiah 14:14). It doesn't work out too well for him—or us. The capstone of God's creation is Adam and Eve, "in our image, to be like us" (Genesis 1:26). Misery loves company; Lucifer tells Eve there's more than the garden. "God knows…you will be like God" (Genesis 3:5). Reaching for more, they become like Lucifer, not God; corrupt their DNA; and produce children in their image. Identity theft takes a human face in Eden.

God gives us a new identity. Ever been in an auto accident? You may think your car is permanently damaged and should go to the wrecking yard, but time in a body shop with hammering, sanding, new parts, and fresh paint sends it back on the road again as good as new. Not quite—underneath the shine, hidden damage remains that only an expert will see.

A spiritual car wreck in Eden permanently damages our spiritual DNA. The image of God in humans is damaged, but is it a total loss? Does God need to start over, or can He repair the damage? Paul describes God's repair of our DNA: "If anyone is in Christ, the new creation has come: The old has gone, the new is here! (2 Corinthians 5:17, NIV). On the surface, we look shiny and new, but the hidden damage to our DNA remains, leaving us vulnerable to spiritual hacking.

God protects our new identity. Trolls, masquerading as trustworthy entities, *phish* the internet, seeking sensitive information they can steal. Hit the wrong key or open the wrong attachment, and they're in; our identity is stolen. LifeLock's guarantee to prevent theft comes with an admission: Should our identity be stolen, the company will spend up to a million dollars restoring it. Should our spiritual identity be breached, God promises to help repair the damage.

When we're in Christ, God's LifeLock is downloaded and cannot be breached. Three Biblical visuals help personalize our security. Peter tells us phishing attempts never stop as the devil "prowls around like a roaring lion, looking for someone to devour" (1 Peter 5:8). Chilling! Another visual is in a conversation about Lucifer's failure to steal Job's identity; he complains God has "put a wall of protection around him" (Job 1:10). Perhaps the most striking difference between commercial LifeLock and God's LifeLock is given by Jesus; commercial software can be hacked, but God's can't. "Don't store up treasures here on earth…where thieves break in and steal. Store your treasures in heaven, where…thieves do not break in and steal" (Matthew 6:19-20). God protects our identity.

We worry about personal identity theft, spending money for security, yet we still feel insecure. Our new identity in Christ comes with God's personal guarantee. In *Finding Truth: 5 Principles for Unmasking Atheism, Secularism, and Other God Substitutes*, Nancy Pearcey said,

> **"Those who don't get their identity from a transcendent Creator will get it from something in creation."**

I BELIEVE IN YOU

Luke, my fourteen-year-old grandson, was playing Pony League baseball and having a good season, catching and batting third. Near season's end, his coach missed one game, leaving the assistant in charge. Following warmups, Luke saw on the lineup he was batting fourth instead of third and asked the coach why. His reply was, "I believe in you." As he went back to the dugout, Luke was fuming and didn't take it as a compliment.

Belief based on observation. The coach had no rapport with or respect of the players and that, coupled with Luke's youth, likely triggered the negative response. Coach had a different perspective as he'd observed his play and based his decision on what he'd seen throughout the season. A brief explanation for the change rather than saying, "I believe in you" would have been better. The change was based on observation

Belief without observation. Many startup companies fail, not for lack of great ideas or enthusiasm, but for lack of the right people. Prospects are vetted via resumé and background checks; any employer who hires based on gut feelings is foolish and has a better than 50 percent chance of failing.

Would we choose a fugitive from justice to lead a nation, a coward to defeat an oppressive enemy, or an impulsive and uneducated man to launch a worldwide movement? Of course not, but God did more than once!

Belief based on faith. Let's consider three examples when God says "I believe in you" when no one else did. Moses knows the best Egypt has to offer but commits a murder and becomes a fugitive, trading palace privileges for a lonely life tending sheep for decades until God shows up and says, "I am sending you to Pharaoh. You must lead my people Israel out of Egypt… I will be with you" (Exodus 3:10, 12). God convinces Moses "I believe in you," and the rest is history.

Israel is on the verge of starvation as the Midianites took all their food; they cry to God for help, and it comes from the least likely source. Gideon has a small measure of grain and is threshing it at the bottom of a wine press to prevent it from being taken. Imagine his shock when an angel says, "Mighty hero, the Lord is with you!" His cynical response prompts the angel to say, "Go with the strength you have, and rescue Israel from the Midianites. I am sending you!" How: "I will be with you. And you will destroy the Midianites as if you were fighting against one man" (Judges 6:11-16). Gideon finally realizes God believes in him and with only 300 men routs a powerful army.

Religion in Israel has a long, stable history until Jesus is introduced as "The Lamb of God who takes away the sin of the world!" (John 1:29). It's definitely a new idea and faces challenges as a startup business. Jesus is a charismatic leader but needs a team to make it work, and picks men no competent CEO would have chosen—fishermen and others without any leadership experience. Walking by the shore He sees Peter and Andrew casting their nets and calls, "Come, follow me, and I will show you how to fish for people!" (Matthew 4:19). They're not picked for their resumés, but Jesus is saying, "I believe in you."

A Pause To Refresh

The common denominator in each example is a reminder that when God says, "I believe in you," He can make it happen. His choice has nothing to do with our abilities but everything to do with His ability to mold us into productive people. It's powerful when God says,

"I believe in YOU!"

GOING FOR GOLD

The Olympic flame is extinguished; the stadium is dark. For millions, the games are over, but untold thousands are beginning a four-year quest for a berth in the next games—one earned through training even when they don't feel like it, their bodies hurt, and their friends are having fun. They're competing for a spot in the next Olympics.

Imagine you're a first-generation Christian. What do you need to know? Imagine Paul as he reaches into their experience to illustrate the faith life. Perhaps it's an Olympic year, and he draws on the images of the games to illustrate first-century truths for Christians through the ages. "We are surrounded by such a huge crowd of witnesses to the life of faith, let us strip off every weight that slows us down, especially the sin that so easily trips us up. And let us run with endurance the race God has set before us...by keeping our eyes on Jesus, the champion who initiates and perfects our faith" (Hebrews 12:1-2).

What does it mean? Faith life is 24/7/365. One-hundred-meter dashes are exciting and quick; a marathon is long and lonely. It tests the runner's will to go on when he hits the wall and the end isn't in sight. Sprinters aren't good marathon runners; marathon runners aren't good sprinters. Faith life is a marathon, and we're to "run with endurance" seven days a week.

If it doesn't work on Tuesday while awaiting test results that may bring bad news, it doesn't work on Sunday. Time to revisit our training.

Is uphill not downhill. Athletes in the ancient games ran naked; that's not permitted today, but today's runners don the bare minimum. Marathon runners aren't overweight, nor do they carry weights when they run; extra weight makes it harder to keep running to the finish line. We're to "strip off every weight that slows us down."

Shedding weight is an uphill struggle and begins with a decision followed by action. Our weights may be friends, a job requiring long hours and deception, a bad habit, or an addiction, slowing us down until we decide to drop it. We'll like what we see when seeing ourselves in God's mirror.

Is forward looking. Watching little girls' first year of soccer is interesting. Decked out in their uniforms, they take to the field, but as the game proceeds, some are distracted, stopping to look at a flower, hug a teammate, or wave to Mom. Distractions are everywhere; to maintain focus, keep our eyes on Jesus who shows us the way.

Is lonely at times but we're not alone. Toward the end of a marathon, runners feel exhausted and alone, but they get new energy as the crowd cheers when they enter the arena. Remember, "we are surrounded by such a huge crowd of witnesses to the life of faith." Days when you feel exhausted, alone, or abandoned by God, picture yourself entering a stadium seeing Noah, Moses, or Abraham, men who finished their marathon, on their feet cheering, "You can do it!"

A Pause To Refresh

In the games, everyone wants the gold and trains hard, giving all, knowing only three percent of participants receive a gold medal. God invites each of us to join other team members in the Life of Faith Games. Decide to join, commit to spiritual disciplines, and keep focus on Jesus who shows the way. Unlike the Olympic games, where few get the gold, in God's sight everyone is gold. Although "the fastest runner doesn't always win the race" (Ecclesiastes 9:11), God urges us to

Go for His gold.

WHEN YOUR WORLD FALLS APART

Horatio Spafford had a family, a successful law practice, and considerable commercial properties, but in the spring of 1871 his son contracted pneumonia and died. Later that same year, the Great Chicago fire destroyed his buildings. In 1873, his business was recovering and he planned a family trip to England, where he would travel with his friend, evangelist D. L. Moody. Passage was booked, but a business emergency required his presence; he stayed behind and sent his family ahead.

Four days into the journey, another ship hit their ship and in twelve minutes it sank. News of the sinking reached Chicago, but there was no word on the fate of his family until he received a telegram from his wife. "Saved alone, what shall I do?" He boarded the next ship to Europe. Late at night after a few days at sea, the captain invited Spafford to his cabin and informed him they were over the spot where the other ship went down.

Standing alone on the deck in the cold dark night, looking at the rough seas, he began forming words for a great hymn of comfort: "When peace like a river, attendeth my way, When sorrows like sea billows roll; Whatever my lot, Thou has taught me to say, It is well, it is well with my soul." How can anyone respond like this when tragedy strikes?

Perspective: he's not the first. Perhaps during the time between the loss of his children and standing on the deck, he'd taken time to reflect on Job, a man who'd lost everything. In the course of twenty-four hours, Job receives devastating news—everything except his wife is lost in a series of tragedies. It gets worse; his body is covered with boils. It's important we know we're not the first.

Pattern. Job suffers alone until three *friends* arrive to comfort him. They're shocked into silence by his plight but soon recover, and in a series of self-righteous speeches, conclude Job is getting what he deserves. His wife joins the cabal with, "Are you still trying to maintain your integrity? Curse God and die" (Job 2:9). When someone close to us experiences a tragedy, how do we react? At first, we're shocked, but soon think we have to say something to comfort our friends. Job's wife and friends bring comfort with their presence, *not* their words. Cry with a friend. Don't try to explain why.

Promise. Job doesn't know why, but he knows God is just; "Should we accept only good things from the hand of God and never anything bad? So in all this, Job said nothing wrong" (Job 2:10). When all the speeches blaming Job are done, God lets everyone know Job is just and rewards his faithfulness.

In the last moments Jesus is with the disciples, He says, "Peace I leave with you; my peace I give you. I do not give to you as the world gives. Do not let your hearts be troubled and do not be afraid" (John 14:27, NIV). It worked for Job, the disciples, and Spafford, but will it work today?

A young mother faced surgery; the prognosis was less than 50 percent chance of survival. Her biggest concern wasn't her health, but her two small children. Just prior to surgery, we shared, "Don't worry about anything; instead, pray about everything. Tell God what you need and thank him for all he has done. Then you will experience God's peace, which exceeds anything we can understand" (Philippians 4:6-7). We told her to then claim the promise. The next day, she said, "As we were approaching the OR doors, I felt a peace I had never felt before." It was well with her soul. "When sorrows like sea billows roll,"

Is it well with your soul?

WARRIOR DOWN

The intercom crackled, Radar announced, "Incoming," and everyone sprang into action. A small chopper landed, and medical teams began treating the wounded as they were transported to the hospital. The zany cast of "M*A*S*H," near the front lines of the Korean War, provided laughter to TV audiences while showing a major improvement in rescuing and treating wounded warriors.

Vietnam provided a ringside seat to treating wounded. Choppers called Dustoff were flown by pilots with ice water in their veins. The call "Dustoff" sent crews running to the choppers, frequently flying into live fire zones risking their own lives to pick up the wounded. When a plane was shot down, all air assets were redirected to efforts to rescue the downed pilot.

"Never leave anyone behind" is in the DNA of our warfighters, beginning with learning how to carry a wounded comrade. More than one Medal of Honor has been earned by a warrior going into hostile fire, ignoring their own safety, to protect a wounded comrade until help arrived. Leaving the wounded behind to save one's self is considered an act of cowardice.

The responsibility of a soldier to the wounded illustrates our responsibilities to fellow believers in our faith walk. Paul admonishes us to "gear up" in God's armor; our battle isn't "against flesh-and-blood enemies, but against…authorities of the unseen world, against mighty powers in this dark world, and against evil spirits in the heavenly places" (Ephesians 6:12).

We sing, "Onward Christian soldiers, marching as to war," but when "someone is caught in a sin," we can look the other way, quarantine them to protect ourselves, activate the prayer chain to pray for them, or step into the line of fire beside them. Sadly, the statement, "The church is the only army who kills their own wounded" describes the reaction of many. When the word *warrior down* is heard in the church, our orders are: leave no one behind; "restore that person" (Galatians 6:1, NIV). No exceptions or deciding someone doesn't deserve our help! God's restoration plan:

Don't send a boy to do a man's job. The instruction to "you who are spiritual" (Galatians 6:1, NASB) indicates the task is for mature, not young, believers. When answering a *warrior down* call, we're like a Dustoff crew, entering a live fire zone. Be alert; the enemy of our soul lies in wait to thwart rescue and trap the rescuer, so "watch yourselves, or you also may be tempted" (Galatians 6:1, NIV).

Find your gentle voice. The wounded need no condemnation from us; they're already condemning themselves. Approach them "gently and humbly help." They need someone to come alongside, lift them up, and carry them like a wounded soldier as we "Share each other's burdens" (Galatians 6:1-2). Those who refuse to get their hands dirty may criticize those who do. Jesus endures withering criticism by the self-righteous for his efforts to rescue sinners; we can expect the same from some.

Leave your high horse in the barn. "If you think you are too important to help someone, you are only fooling yourself. You are not that important" (Galatians 6:1). Jesus doesn't consider Himself too important to wash the disciples' feet. Restoring the sinner requires we jettison any holier-than-thou attitudes, get out of our holy huddle, step onto the devil's turf, and make every effort to rescue the wounded brother.

Wounded soldiers know they won't be left behind. When wounded in spiritual battle, believers need to know the church will

Leave no one behind!

GENERAL RULES...EXCEPTIONS

It was Halloween, a night I don't particularly like, but we had the usual stash, including some yummy chocolate. My wife had to work, leaving me in charge of the distribution. Before leaving, she put a table by the door with a bowl of candy, but when I looked, there was not a single chocolate morsel! ARRRGH, it was gonna be a long night! I was contemplating turning off the lights and going to the back of the house, but a steady stream of big and little goblins began.

A Kodak moment (digital moment) occurred near the end of the evening as a group of little goblins were at our door getting candy as parents stood nearby. I mentioned to the parents, "My wife didn't leave me a single piece of chocolate." Looking down, a little girl about three said, "You can have one of mine," as her tiny hand held out a small Twix bar. Kleenex time!

A general rule. When I was young, most parents believed "Children are to be seen, not heard." They don't have enough life experiences to inject their ideas into adult conversations, so enforcement by some parents was strict. On that Halloween night, a three-year-old girl spoke up and taught me, the parents, and other little goblins a powerful lesson about sharing.

Exceptions to the rule. Jesus is surrounded by His "Secret Service" (disciples) during His travel when some parents press close, wanting Him to bless their little ones, but they are pushed back. Don't you know children are to be seen, not heard? Seeing this, the disciples are reprimanded. "Then He took the children in His arms and placed His hands on their heads and blessed them" (Mark 10:13-16). Exception: Jesus has time for everyone, even children.

A large crowd gathers to hear Jesus; late in the day, His disciples say it's time to send the crowd away. It's dinner time, and there are no food trucks nearby. Imagine the shock when He says, "You feed them." A young boy, the only one with food, offers to share his lunch. Any who reads this story the first time today likely will have the same reaction, "What is that among so many?" Jesus teams up with the boy and teaches a lesson that is still being taught today. A bag lunch in the boy's hand feeds one, but in Jesus's hand it feeds 5,000+. Exception: Whatever we have is enough when we put it in God's hands! (Matthew 14:15-21).

The principle that children are to be seen and not heard is captured with: "'Honor your father and mother.' This is the first commandment with a promise" (Ephesians 6:2). Paul confronts this in practical terms with Timothy, who is appointed to lead a congregation of new believers. We don't know his age, but reading between the lines, it appears the elders may think he's too young.

It's likely that word reaches Paul concerning the boy getting too big for his britches. Paul, in a letter to Timothy, outlines instructions concerning important doctrines for the church and the relationships between believers. Knowing he's

A Pause To Refresh

likely to get pushback and criticism from the elders, he adds, "Teach these things and insist that everyone learn them. Don't let anyone think less of you because you are young" (1 Timothy 4:11-12). Exception: God's calling doesn't have minimum age limits.

Society maintains balance—everything and everyone in their place, but Isaiah (11:6) sees a future day when "the wolf and the lamb will live together; the leopard will lie down with the baby goat, the calf and the yearling will be safe with the lion, and

A little child will lead them all."

SPEAK TRUTH TO POWER

Imagine being ushered into the office of the most powerful man in the country on a mission to deliver a message he will *not* like. What do you do? Now visualize Moses, played by Charlton Heston, entering the palace of the most ruthless dictator in the world to deliver a message that can get him killed. Does he tell him the truth or what the king wants to hear?

Speaking Truth to Power…the mandate. The ancient world is ruled by kings and dictators who make all the rules; dissent can be hazardous to one's health. Moses, a fugitive from Egypt, is minding his own business when God gives him a mission (Exodus 3): Return to Egypt to tell the king God says, "Let my people go!" He's afraid but delivers the message to a king who thinks of himself as a god, and the response is, "I do not know the Lord and I will not let Israel go" (Exodus 5:2). Game on—"god" against God!

David, the king of Israel, commits adultery, arranges the husband's death in battle, takes the woman as his wife, and is living happily ever after until God sends Nathan, a prophet who tells a story about a man to make God's point rather than an in-your-face approach. David gets the point of the story, then Nathan says, "You are that man!" (2 Samuel 12:7). God knows!

A Pause To Refresh

Old Testament prophets frequently confront kings of Israel with "This is what the LORD says" (Isaiah 45:11). On numerous occasions, Jesus speaks against the religiously powerful and ultimately the political ruler of the land. The apostles and those who come after them speak up. Paul says, "I speak the truth in Christ" (Romans 9:1, NIV).

Speaking truth and consequences. It's not always popular and can get you killed, but it's the right thing to do. Jehoshaphat agrees to join Ahab in battle but asks what God says. Ahab summons his 400 prophets who tell him what he wants to hear. But Jehoshaphat asks, "Is there not also a prophet of the LORD here?" Ahab answers, "There is one more man who could consult the LORD for us, but I hate him. He never prophesies anything but trouble for me" (1 Kings 22:7-8).

The king of Egypt rejects truth, Egypt is devastated, Israel is born, the political landscape changes. David cries out to God for forgiveness; his sin is forgiven, but the consequences will dog him the rest of his life. Yet he's called a man after God's own heart. God forgives a sinner. When given the opportunity to avoid crucifixion, Jesus speaks truth, is crucified, and rises from the dead, bringing hope and salvation for all. Stephen gives a defense of his faith and is stoned by the powerful.

Speaking truth to power in our world. The first amendment to our constitution says that freedom of speech "shall not be abridged," but say anything contrary to the mainstream, and free speech is labeled hate speech. Gorge Orwell is believed to have said, "During times of universal deceit, telling the truth becomes a revolutionary act." In ancient times, speaking truth to power was outsourced to God's appointed few. No more! God gives each of us that responsibility.

Few get an audience to give our president an earful of truth. Our leaders—local, state, and national—are elected, not appointed. The ballot box is our conduit for speaking truth to political power. Talking the talk speaks only when we walk the walk! Jesus says our works gives power to our words. "Let your good deeds shine out for all to see, so that everyone will praise your heavenly Father" (Matthew 5:16). Our words and interactions with those around us are the best way to

Speak truth to power.

FIRST THINGS FIRST

While holding my first great-granddaughter the day after she was born, I whispered, "Honey, your parents are rookies at this and will be easy to train." Newborns don't come with a how-to manual, warranties, or what-to-do-when instructions; it's on-the-job training! Parents seem anxious to make their babies little adults as quickly as possible, but is that a good thing?

Toward the end of Jesus's ministry, His disciples, believing the Kingdom is imminent, are "arguing about which of them was the greatest" (Mark 9:34). Unable to agree on the pecking order, they ask Jesus, "Who is greatest in the Kingdom of Heaven?" Instead of answering the question directly, He calls "a little child to him and put the child among them" (Matthew 18:1-2). Why?

We frequently read the Gospels and miss an important teaching tool Jesus uses—visuals and stories, the seen (physical) to explain the unseen (spiritual). Why does He use a child? The visual (a child) focuses attention on the truth, "Unless you change and become like little children, you will never enter the kingdom of heaven" (Matthew 18:3, NIV). It's not who will get the corner office; presence is more important than the position. What does it mean to become like a little child?

First things first. Nicodemus, a religious expert, engages Jesus in a conversation with a compliment, but Jesus cuts to the chase, answering the real question before it's asked. "I tell you the truth, unless you are born again, you cannot see the Kingdom of God." Physical life begins with birth. "Humans can reproduce only human life, but the Holy Spirit gives birth to spiritual life. So don't be surprised when I say, 'You must be born again'" (John 3:3, 6-7).

Nourishment is essential. A newborn brings sleep deprivation to parents, crying every couple of hours to let Mom and Dad know a little tummy is empty and in need of nourishment. Parents accept this interruption of their lives as part of the deal, but as babies grow they need solid food.

Spiritual growth follows the same pattern of milk to solid food: "Like newborn babies, you must crave pure spiritual milk so that you will grow into a full experience of salvation" (1 Peter 2:2). Paul chastises the Corinthians for continuing to be bottle babies. "I had to feed you with milk, not with solid food, because you weren't ready for anything stronger" (1 Corinthians 3:2).

Discipline is necessary. We've all been in a store when a five-year-old or a teen throws a fit because they don't get their way. With my dad, such behavior was a bridge too far as he was a firm believer in discipline, but we kids had an alternative view. When we became parents, we understood that "No discipline is enjoyable while it is happening—it's painful! But afterward there will be a peaceful harvest of right living for those who are trained in this way" (Hebrews 12:11). "Wait until your daddy gets home" was the worst thing Mother ever said to us.

A Pause To Refresh

Solomon gives us the divine perspective when he says, "My child, don't reject the LORD's discipline…the LORD corrects those he loves, just as a father corrects a child" (Proverbs 3:11-12).

In personal correspondence with me, Chaplain (LT) Gene Monnin said, "Children ought to be our greatest teachers. We have so much to learn from them about love, loyalty, joy, and peace. Rather than devoting our energies to becoming more like them, sadly we aspire to make them more like us.…The real tragedy, of course, is that we are succeeding." His statement reminds us we need to

Put first things first.

TO BAKE OR NOT TO BAKE

"We reserve the right to refuse service to anyone" signs once were seen at all businesses, but no more. Now, governmental agencies are telling business owners that it's discrimination to refuse service to anyone even if it violates their deeply held faith. Courts are being asked to decide if business owners are free to bake or not to bake.

Religious liberty and Jesus. He offends the religious establishment by saying, "You are looking for a way to kill me, because you have no room for my word" (John 8:37, NIV). He tells his followers, "You will be handed over to the courts and will be flogged with whips in the synagogues. You will stand trial before governors and kings because you are my followers" (Matthew 10:17-18). When brought before Pilate, Jesus doesn't play a Get out of Crucifixion Free card; when dying, He says, "Father, forgive them, for they don't know what they are doing" (Luke 23:34).

Religious liberty in the first century. Jesus tells his followers, "Since they persecuted me, naturally they will persecute you" (John 15:20). The apostles begin teaching, healing the sick, and drawing such crowds the religious establishment was "filled with jealousy" and "arrested the apostles and put them in the public jail" (Acts 5:17-18). God breaks them out of jail. When told to keep their religion to themselves, they respond, "We must obey

A Pause To Refresh

God rather than any human authority" (Acts 5:29) and speak about Jesus anyway, infuriating the religious leaders.

Stephen draws the ire of the establishment, and false witnesses accuse him of hate speech, speaking against the laws of Moses. His response turns the tables; the "leaders were infuriated…and they shook their fists at him in rage…they put their hands over their ears and began shouting. They rushed at him and dragged him out of the city and began to stone him." His last words are, "Lord, don't charge them with this sin!" (Acts 7:54-60).

Religious liberty in the twenty-first century. Bakers say their right to not bake a cake is guaranteed by the Constitution, but any liberty granted by the state can be taken away by the state. In much of the world, being a Christian is the most dangerous thing you can be. A 2017 report by The Center for Studies on New Religions says 90,000 Christians were killed worldwide for their faith; as many as 600 million were denied religious liberty. Images of twenty Egyptian Christians calmly kneeling on a Libyan beach are burned into our consciousness. They were executed because they were followers of Jesus, showing no fear and refusing to deny Christ. Would I be so resolute in my faith? Would you?

Jesus said, "All nations will hate you because you are my followers" (Matthew 10:22). How then shall we live as hostility toward our faith is on the rise? Paul says, "Do all that you can to live in peace with everyone" (Romans 12:18). Should we use the courts to defend our religious liberties? Yes, but understand that any time a court is in session our religious liberty is in jeopardy.

A Pause To Refresh

Will we ever be required to choose between our faith and life? Only God knows, but should it come, remember Jesus's words: "Don't be afraid of those who want to kill your body; they cannot touch your soul. Fear only God, who can destroy both soul and body in hell" (Matthew 10:28).

You want religious liberty? John says it can be found in one source (John 8:36, NIV).

"If the Son sets you free, you will be free indeed."

I CAN'T, CAN I?

The Depression of the 1930s was a bad time to begin a family. Jobs were scarce, millions of men were unemployed and stood in bread lines for food, and some who couldn't find work committed suicide. Despite the bad economy, Dad and Mom began their life together, and in six years had four boys to feed and clothe. Dad refused charity and worked anywhere he could to provide for us.

"I can't" was a non-starter when he gave us a job to do. His response was, "Can't never could do anything!" We learned we could do it, but it was work. I don't recall ever hearing him say, "I can't," regardless of what we needed. I didn't appreciate his wisdom until my own children started saying, "I can't." Jesus and Paul address this issue, teaching what we encounter in life mirrors our walk of faith. We learn there's a bridge between "can't" and "can."

We can't—a natural reaction. Do we say "I can't" because we don't want to do something or because we think it's too hard or beyond our abilities? My dad had been through things more difficult than he asked of us and wouldn't accept "I can't." Jesus addresses the issue of "I can't."

The last evening Jesus is with His disciples, He leaves their heads reeling with some final instructions. Imagine their reaction as He uses a familiar image of a vineyard and its branches to illustrate their inability to accomplish ministry on their own: "Apart from me you can do nothing" (John 15:5).

We encounter this principle every day. I notice my cell phone needs charging so I plug it in, but when I return later, the phone is off. I follow the line down to the outlet and discover the charger isn't properly plugged into the power source. The phone in my hand can't work without power; ministry can't work unless we're drawing power from God's source—Jesus.

We can—a learned attitude. Dad taught us to approach chores with a can-do attitude. The more we succeeded, the more we realized he was right. "I can't" becomes "I can" when I use resources available to me, but it's a learned attitude. Paul says, "I have learned how to be content with whatever I have…I have learned the secret of living in every situation" (Philippians 4:11-12).

If anyone had reasons to say, "I can't," it was the Apostle Paul. He was beaten, shipwrecked, spent time in many jails, accused of blasphemy, and went hungry, yet he continued his ministry. He turns Jesus's words, "apart from me you can do nothing," into a positive: "For I can do everything through Christ, who gives me strength" (Philippians 4:13).

Sure, that worked for Paul, but do you think he ever thought "I can't" to any challenge? If he did, we have no record, but his statement "I have learned" suggests we're not alone. Relying on God's strength is a learning experience with each new challenge.

A friend involved in ministry to deployed troops was about to meet with Green Mountain Coffee to ask for a rather large donation of coffee and asked for suggestions on what to say if they were reluctant. I told him if they hesitated to use Jesus's words, "The Lord has need of it" (Luke 19:31, NASB). He called to let me know they agreed to the donation. I asked, "What did you say to them?" He replied, "I told them God wants us to have this."

If you find yourself thinking you can't do what God asks you to do, ask yourself, "Am I plugged into His power?" When we're plugged into his power,

We can!

WE NEED TO TALK

The phone rang. In even tones my wife said, "When I get home, we need to talk." I answered, "Okay," and spent the afternoon wondering what I had done to warrant the call. She had to know something, or else she wouldn't have had that tone in her voice. She came home, we sat down, and I braced myself to hear what I had done. When she told me what prompted the call, I wasn't at fault—this time! Inwardly I was jumping for joy. It was serious, but it wasn't my fault.

We instinctively react like I did because of conscience, a built-in mechanism that alerts us to the presence of temptation or reminds us when we cross the line. All of us have done things in the past we hide from everyone except ourselves.

Conscience: God's early warning system. The sign "Speed Checked by Radar" tells us our bank account may be in danger if we ignore the speed limit. Conscience is designed to warn us against bad behavior. It may not keep us from doing wrong, but it keeps us from enjoying it.

The Greek word *suneidēsis* (translated *conscience*) means *moral awareness* or *moral conscience*. Some may think conscience is given to Christians to make us miserable, but Paul declares, "Even Gentiles, who do not have God's written law… demonstrate that God's law is written in their hearts, for their own conscience and thoughts either accuse them or tell them they are doing right" (Romans 2:14-15).

Conscience: The devil's playground. Everything we have said, seen, or done is stored on our internal hard drive; it can't be deleted or erased, and it isn't password protected. We may have forgotten, but it's buried in our unconscious.

We do something wrong and seek forgiveness, but we think God behaves like we do—forgives but never forgets what we did. When God forgives, He forgets. "Their sins and lawless acts I will remember no more" (Hebrews 10:17, NIV). God doesn't remind us of forgiven failures. The devil is the "accuser of our brothers and sisters" (Revelation 12:10) and "our great enemy....He prowls around like a roaring lion, looking for someone to devour" (1 Peter 5:8).

On trash day we've all seen someone digging through things we've discarded searching for something useful. Visualize the devil poking through your memory for something from your past he can and will use to torment you. God doesn't remember our sins, and the devil never forgets!

Conscience: Battleground for human behavior. Flip Wilson was wrong; the devil can't make us do it. Many names and adjectives are used to describe the devil, but coward isn't one of them. The Book of Job opens with a conversation between God and the devil, who has "been patrolling the earth, watching everything that's going on" (Job 1:7). He says Job is good only because God protects him; protection is removed, the battle is joined, and in the end God was right. He will say the same about us.

Temptation is as old as Eden when the devil smooth talks Eve. He questions God—"Did God really say," challenges God—"You will not certainly die," and claims God is selfish—"God knows that when you eat from it your eyes will be opened, and you will be like God" (Genesis 3:1-5, NIV). We can't claim Eve's innocence, but we can expect the same approach that God wants us to be miserable when just the opposite is true.

It's more than "You can't eat just one potato chip;" it's about our conscience and whether we'll believe the lie. When we make that mistake the devil hacks our conscience, throws it in our face, and declares,

"Guilty."

THE CLOCK IS TICKING

The San Francisco 49ers were trailing the Arizona Cardinals by four points at the two-minute warning. They were moving the ball smartly down the field. The Niners were on Arizona's three-yard line with one time out remaining and would likely score on the last play of the game, but they needed a touchdown for a win. Everyone in the stadium, press box, and watching on TV saw the end zone clock ticking toward 00.00. There was confusion among the coaches, and by the time they sent in the final play, time had expired. Game over!

Afterward, the coaches said they thought they had more time. Every game has rules and time limits (minutes, periods, and innings), and players know the rules. Life is a game we play by God's rules; He alone knows when our time clock will reach 00.00.

Our clock is ticking. The cry of the newborn in a delivery room brings joy; it also signals the beginning of the end as the tiny heart starts ticking down to 00.00. Jesus tells the story of a farmer whose hard work is rewarded with a bumper crop, more than his existing barns will hold. He decides to build bigger barns for his crops, retire, and take it easy. God says, "You fool! You will die this very night. Then who will get everything you worked for?" (Luke 12:20).

The story teaches that time is God's gift, and how we use it is important both now and for eternity. Jesus says we're to use the time we have wisely; "As long as it is day, we must do the works of Him who sent me. Night is coming, when no one can work" (John 9:4, NIV).

God controls our clock. Occasionally a game is stopped, and the timekeeper is instructed to put more time on the clock. A Roman officer's highly valued slave is near death; he sends Jewish leaders to Jesus to request healing. As Jesus approaches, the soldier says Jesus can say the word and the servant will be healed. When they return home, they find that Jesus had healed the slave, putting more time on his clock (Luke 7:1-10).

A medical test for a different issue raised red flags concerning my heart; tests indicated the need for surgery even though I had no symptoms. My heart was stopped during the procedure to repair the main artery that was 98 percent blocked. While my heart was stopped, repairs were made, and restarted; God added time to my clock.

Our clock will reach 00.00. The coaches can see the game clock but were busy trying to win the game and forgot the clock was steadily ticking down. They lost a game they could have won. We don't have a visible time clock, yet many push the envelope, hoping at the last minute to get right with God. How often do we hear, "He died unexpectedly?"

Jesus puts our time on earth in perspective; think long term as our time on earth is limited and eternity is certain. "You are seeing things merely from a human point of view, not from God's....If you try to hang on to your life, you will lose it. But if you give up your life for my sake…you will save it" (Mark 8:33, 35).

Only God knows how much time is left on our clock. "Today when you hear His voice, don't harden your hearts as Israel did when they rebelled, when they tested me in the wilderness" (Hebrews 3:7-8). Life comes with a limited warranty; the only time I have is now, because

My clock is ticking.

FLYING BLIND

As he sits at his radar console, the Air Traffic Controller is responsible for the safety of the pilots, passengers, and airplanes flying through his sector. The pilot can't see what the controller sees and is taught to trust and follow the controller's instructions. A pilot who ignores a controller's direction is flying blind and is headed for trouble!

The relationship between a pilot and controller illustrates our faith journey. "For we walk by faith, not by sight" (2 Corinthians 5:7, NASB). God lays out the course we're to follow: "Whether you turn to the right or to the left, your ears will hear a voice behind you, saying, 'This is the way; walk in it'" (Isaiah 30:21, NIV). The Holy Spirit is God's controller to guide us on our faith journey; we can't see what's ahead, but God can. Ignore His directions and we're flying blind.

Flying blind is a choice. "There is a path before each person that seems right" (Proverbs 14:12). We're frequently like the pilot who sees sunshine and not the bad weather the controller sees, and we choose to go by what we see. Abram is a case study in following God's direction "go to the land I will show you" (Genesis 12:1). Months later, he arrives in Canaan with his considerable livestock, servants, and family. God tells him this is the land; he builds two altars.

A Pause To Refresh

His travels through the land reveal "a severe famine struck the land of Canaan." Decision time: his wealth is in livestock; no grass means no cows and no wealth. Do you believe God or your eyes? He sees others heading to Egypt, so he goes "down to Egypt, where he lived as a foreigner" (Genesis 12:10).

Flying blind has consequences. "But it ends in death" (Proverbs 14:12). He survives; no big deal. God's promises are land specific: "the land I will show you," not Egypt. Deceit: before arriving, he tells his wife to say she's his sister to keep Pharaoh from killing him. If God can't feed his livestock, how can he protect him from the king? Sarah is taken to the harem, he's given gifts; life is good until his deceit is uncovered. Following a severe tongue lashing, he's deported.

He heads back to Canaan where the famine continues and the need for feed is greater since "Pharaoh gave Abram many...sheep, goats, cattle, male and female donkeys, male and female servants, and camels" (Genesis 12:16). He gets a second chance to allow God to provide, but he returns with the Hagar virus. Hagar is given to Sarai as her maid and becomes the mother of Ishmael. The sons of Ishmael and sons of Abraham are still fighting.

I grew up on a farm. Livestock didn't offer to skip eating during droughts; they expected feed every day. Out of his own experience, Paul declares, "My God will meet all your needs according to the riches of his glory in Christ Jesus" (Philippians 4:19, NIV). Unlike store coupons, God's promises never expire.

Joe was living the American Dream: a family, a good paying job in his chosen field of engineering, a nice home in the suburbs, a promising career. One day he told his family God had called him to ministry. He sold his home, moved to Dallas, enrolled in seminary, and began looking for work during a recession. Weeks, then months, passed, reserves dwindled, and decision time had arrived. Some friends suggested he return to California, but Joe said, "God called me, and I'm going to trust him." He finished seminary and was a missionary in Latin America. He followed God rather than his own instincts and learned

Where God guides, He provides.

Special Devotions for Special Days

New Year's Day
Mother's Day
Father's Day
Thanksgiving
Christmas

THE REST OF THE STORY

"Hello, Americans, this is Paul Harvey. Stand by for news." Millions tuned in daily during World War II to hear Paul Harvey's distinctive voice and style. On May 10, 1976, "The Rest of the Story" segment became a separate broadcast, presenting details and significance of the news, connecting the news stories, and ending with "And now you know the rest of the story. Paul Harvey. Good Day!"

Headline news. While watching TV, we might hear, "We interrupt this broadcast to bring breaking news," then following the news alert, "We now return to…," after we've missed a crucial part of the whodunit story.

The greatest news story ever told was noticed by some star gazers and shepherds who heard the first musical birth announcement. The announcement didn't interrupt the lives of those busy eking out an existence, and without social media, they got news by word of mouth!

Every year, that news headline captivates and consumes enormous amount of our energy, but once Christmas is over, the decorations are put away, the countdown to the next Christmas begins. We recall the headlines, sing carols, then turn attention to other things. Have you noticed Jesus is still a baby and never gets out of the manger?

A Pause To Refresh

The Rest of the Story. The story wasn't trending on social media. For thirty years, the pages are blank except a few mentions: three Magi, an Egyptian trip, and the Baby, now twelve, stunning the temple bigshots with His wisdom. John the Baptist's proclamation, "Look! The Lamb of God who takes away the sin of the world!" (John 1:29) signals He's now a man on a mission from God.

We have something Jesus's contemporaries didn't have: 20/20 hindsight. To us, the Gospel narratives read like a mystery novel where we already know the ending, but for the participants, every day was an adventure. Jesus calls, "Come, follow me, and I will show you how to fish for people!" (Matthew 4:19). Peter and Andrew are the first of twelve chosen for the mission.

Everywhere they go crowds gather. Jesus touches the sick, feeds the hungry, casts out demons, and talks about the Kingdom of Heaven. Word spreads, and in short order, the religious establishment takes note, sending spies to keep an eye on this upstart rabbi who is generating so much excitement.

They feel threatened and begin challenging Jesus, His teaching, and His miracles at every opportunity, but His popularity continues to grow until, in desperation, a plan is devised to arrest Him and convince the Romans to crucify Him. The arrest is made, and a sham trial condemns Him to death. On Friday, He's crucified, dies, and is buried in a borrowed tomb. His mission failed, but did it?

Sabbath begins with the religious leaders congratulating themselves for eliminating a populist threat to their power.

A Pause To Refresh

Jesus's followers scatter, the city is quiet until Sunday morning. Women come to the tomb and find Jesus missing. They're told "He isn't here! He is risen from the dead, just as he said would happen" (Matthew 28:6). Imagine the panic among those who engineered the crucifixion when they realize God played His trump card: resurrection.

Making the connection. The birth of Jesus and the resurrection occur years apart, and we treat them as two distinct and separate events. But they are connected. Mary is told, "he will save his people from their sins" (Matthew 1:21). Baby Jesus can't save anyone; neither can a dead Jesus! The Gospel narrative makes the connection: without the manger, the resurrection is impossible; without the resurrection, the manger is unnecessary. You can't have one without the other. "And now you know

The rest of the story. Good Day!"

A MOTHER'S HEART

I'm sitting behind the screen at a Little League game of ten-year-old boys when one of my grandsons comes to bat. His best buddy is pitching for the other team, so Luke gives him a big smile as he steps into the box. His buddy goes into his windup and delivers his first pitch, a high inside fastball that hits Luke in the neck. In spite of the rules, his mother is on the field almost by the time he hits the ground. Moms don't need no stinking rules when their baby is hurt!

What happens when a little one gets an owie? Ninety percent of the time, they run right past Dad, dissolving into a puddle of tears in the safety of Mom's arms. Sorry, Dads, it's the mother hen, not the rooster, who covers baby chicks with her wings. The natural instinct of a child to turn to Mom for comfort instead of Dad continues into adulthood. A mother will get a call from her adult son, "Mom, my car won't start," even though Mom knows less about mechanics than he does.

Occasionally during a football game, the camera pans to big men dressed for battle, looking like someone you don't want as an enemy. But when they realize they're on camera, they smile, wave, and say, "Hi Mom!" I've never seen one say, "Hi Dad!"

A Pandora Jewelry ad (April 2015) illustrated the mother-child bond with six children ages three to nine. They were blindfolded and taken into a room where the mothers were lined up. One by one, each was asked to identify their mom by feeling only their hands and face. The anxious looks on the moms' faces turned to smiles and hugs as each child correctly identified their mom. That mysterious bond exists between mother and child because the child has heard and felt the comforting beat of Mom's heart from inside.

A unique birth announcement. Shepherds are startled and terrified as the night sky is illuminated and they see an angel of the Lord. After the angels calm the frightened shepherds, they make a musical birth announcement: A Savior/Messiah has been born in Bethlehem. Hurrying to Bethlehem, the shepherds find Jesus with His mother and father, tell their story, and get two reactions. Most who heard their story "were amazed. But Mary treasured up all these things and pondered them in her heart" (Luke 2:18-19, NIV). No doubt Mary thinks back over the nine months. Is this the meaning of the angel's words, "He will be very great and will be called the Son of the Most High" (Luke 1:32)?

Expectant mothers identify with Mary's thoughts and emotions of new life developing inside, feeling the first flutter of life, and then donkey-like kicks inside her. Technology gives us a ringside seat to see what had been a mystery to all but God, confirming the Psalmist's words: "You watched me as I was being formed in utter seclusion, as I was woven together in the dark of the womb. You saw me before I was born" (Psalm 139:15-16).

At birth, the physical cord is cut, allowing the baby to function outside the protective environment of the mother's womb, but the invisible cord of a mother's protective love for her baby is never severed. If you wonder what God's love looks like, observe a mother when her child is in need or in trouble, and do not get in the way when a child cries, "Mom!" She will deny her own needs and sacrifice anything to shelter her children, even from their own mistakes. We might paraphrase an ancient proverb: "The name [Mom] is a strong fortress; children run to [her] and feel safe" (Proverbs 18:10).

It's a mother's heart that prompts big burly men to smile at the camera and say,

"Hi, Mom!"

MY DAD IS...

Yu Xukang, a single dad in China, had a twelve-year-old son who was severely disabled with twisted arms and legs and a hunched back. Local schools refused to admit his son because of his disability. Another school would take him, but it was miles away. There were no school buses, and Yu didn't have a car.

In spite of his disabilities, Yu's dream was that one day his son could go to college. He had to go to school first, but how? Yu built a special basket to carry his son on his back. He rose at 5:00 AM to feed him and prepare a lunch; he carried his son four and a half miles to school, then returned so he could work. At the end of the day, he walked back to school to bring his son home, a total of eighteen miles a day. Yu estimated he's carried Xiao 1600 miles through rocky paths and up steep hills. The boy could tell his classmates, "My dad is bigger than your dad!"

Yu's story made the news, the local government announced it would rent a room to the dad, and the school stepped up, arranging to take boarding students like Xiao. This father illustrates a theme woven into the fabric of Scripture—God, our heavenly Father, is invisible, so Scripture uses visible family relationships to give God a face, heart, hands, and feet.

When life is hard. Issues we face daily vary from S, M, L, XL, XXL, to "You Gotta Be Kidding Me," causing us to feel overwhelmed and helpless. Few problems we face are as big as Israel faces on their forty-year wilderness journey: they run out of food and water and are attacked; their actual survival is in doubt. Near the end of their journey Moses says, "In the wilderness...you saw how the Lord your God carried you, just as a man carries his son, in all the way which you have walked until you came to this place" (Deuteronomy 1:31, NASB). God was bigger than their problems; He's bigger than ours.

Meeting our needs. We didn't have much when I was a child, but when I needed something, I said, "Dad I need...," never doubting he would make it happen. It wasn't until I became a dad that I understood some of the things I needed may have been hard, but he never said, "Son, we can't afford that." Think beyond the need to the provider. "Your Father knows what you need before you ask him" (Matthew 6:8, NIV) and "each day he carries us in his arms" (Psalm 68:19). He can afford it!

Our entire journey. A dad's work is never done. I have adult children and grandchildren who've learned a lot since their teens. Although they don't need me to tie their shoes or button their shirt, it's humbling when one asks Dad or Gramps for his opinion. They know, regardless of their age, that Dad still has a minimum of twenty-five years more of life experiences. Israel goes through a lot of self-inflicted suffering when God reminds them: "I have cared for you since you were born. Yes, I carried you before you were born. I will be your God...until your hair is white with age. I made you, and I will care for you. I will carry you" (Isaiah 46:3-4).

A Pause To Refresh

All little boys, including Xaio's classmates, think their dad is the greatest, but after seeing his dad bring him to school on his back every day, they'd likely agree his dad is the greatest. In a conversation with His disciples (John 10:29, NIV), Jesus settles all arguments or disputes when He said,

"My Father...is greater than all."

GRATITUDE IS...

A philosopher and keen observer, Dr. Seuss, touches one of the thorny issues of life with:

> When you think things are bad,
>
> when you feel sour and blue,
>
> when you start to get mad...
>
> you should do what I do!
>
> Just tell yourself, Duckie,
>
> you're really quite lucky!
>
> Some people are much more...
>
> oh, ever so much more...
>
> oh, muchly much-much more
>
> unlucky than you.

Life is a journey of twists, turns, ups, downs, good news, and bad news. Faith informs our reactions to daily life. It's easy to smile and be cheerful when good news comes our way, but how we handle the bad provides a window into our soul. Does our faith make a difference when the chips are down?

Problems are a fact of life. Some promote the idea faith is lived out in a spiritual Camelot where it's all sunshine and roses, but God doesn't put us in a witness protection program. Jesus shatters that pipe dream. "For He gives His sunlight to both the evil and the good, and He sends rain on the just and the unjust alike" (Matthew 5:45).

When problems come our way, the lyrics of the Negro spiritual "Nobody Knows the Trouble I've Seen" plays in our heads, but those problems pale by comparison to Paul's experiences. Rather than complain, he considers it a badge of honor, listing the trouble he's seen because of his faith—whipped numerous times, faced death over and over, given thirty-nine lashes five times, beaten with rods, stoned, in three shipwrecks, adrift at sea, traveled many miles, faced danger from rivers, robbers, Jews, and Gentiles, was hungry, thirsty, and cold (2 Corinthians 11:23-27). Dare we compare our troubles with Paul's? Problems are a fact of life but…

Problems are opportunities. Lemons make great lemonade, but not until they've been squeezed. Zig Ziglar's dad died when he was six, leaving his mother to raise eleven children during the Depression, decades before any government programs for the needy. His mom raised her kids to believe that both she and God loved them and to practice saying please and thank you. He said in spite of hardships, gratitude made their lives enjoyable. As an adult, he popularized the phrase "an attitude of gratitude." Cicero said, "Gratitude is not only the greatest of virtues, but the parent of all the others."

Problems squeezed the lemonade of joy and gratitude from Paul's spirit as opportunities for sharing. Take a moment to reflect on the problems he experienced as we capture his expressions: "Give thanks in all circumstances" (1 Thessalonians 5:18, NIV); "Giving thanks always and for everything" (Ephesians 5:20, ESV); "In everything by prayer and supplication with thanksgiving let your requests be made known to God" (Philippians 4:6, NASB); "And be thankful" (Colossians 3:15, NIV).

Problems—we're not alone. In the old spiritual, the words "Nobody knows the trouble I've seen," are followed by the words "Nobody knows but Jesus." We have: His presence—"I am with you always" (Matthew 28:20), His promise—"When you go through deep waters, I will be with you. When you go through rivers of difficulty, you will not drown" (Isaiah 43:2), and His people—"Therefore, since we are surrounded by such a huge crowd of witnesses to the life of faith, let us strip off every weight that slows us down" (Hebrews 12:1).

Gratitude is an attitude. When bad things happen, Dr. Seuss says we can either

Show our grump or our gratitude!

THE NIGHT BEFORE

The night before Christmas triggers a new normal in activities. Procrastinating husbands crowd the stores to grab something (anything) for their wives; exhausted parents anxiously wait for the last order from Amazon Prime to arrive; children full of excitement may be snug in their beds but want morning to come.

Meanwhile, families stuck in bumper-to-bumper traffic aren't experiencing "Joy to the World" emotions; merchants are counting the money after businesses close, hoping the receipts are enough. First responders and ER personnel are on duty, hoping for an uneventful night. The significance of Christmas Eve has been co-opted by an avalanche of other things.

Let's mentally step back to the first Christmas Eve and visit some of the players. "In those days Caesar Augustus issued a decree that a census should be taken" (Luke 2:1, NIV). Tax collectors are happy as they'll have a list of everyone in their region and know how much to collect for the king plus their commission. They're unaware of what's about to happen.

"And everyone went to their own town to register" (Luke 2:2, NIV). Innkeepers post "No Vacancy" signs, and all spare rooms are filled with relatives. There is no lodging anywhere. Imagine the nose-to-tail donkey traffic and huge crowds walking along the dusty roads, grumbling about the traffic and registering for the tax man. Somewhere in the throng, a very pregnant teenager and her husband make their way toward Bethlehem. Most likely they're anxious but unaware of what the night will bring.

Mary and Joseph arrive and learn they'll have to sleep on the streets as no lodging is available until they're offered a stall in a smelly barn. Imagine teenage Joseph's panic when Mary goes into labor. I suspect other women in town came to assist when "She gave birth to her firstborn son…and laid him in a manger." The shepherds come to see the baby, then "…told everyone what had happened and what the angel had said to them about this child…Mary kept all these things in her heart and thought about them often" (Luke 2:7-16-19).

Outside Bethlehem, shepherds huddle by the campfire trying to keep warm on the long night shift guarding their flocks. They are terrified when an angel of the Lord appears among them, and the radiance of the Lord's glory surrounds them. They're the first to hear "The Savior…has been born today in Bethlehem….you will find a baby wrapped snugly in strips of cloth, lying in a manger." An angel choir joins in, singing, "Glory to God in highest heaven, and peace on earth to those with whom God is pleased." Leaving their flocks behind, the shepherds head to Jerusalem in search of the Savior (Luke 2:8-15).

Thousands of miles away, wise men studying the stars are the first to realize the significance of what they're seeing. They load their camels, pack gifts fit for a king, and hit the road to Jerusalem. Upon arrival, they ask, "Where is the newborn king of the Jews? We saw his star as it rose, and we have come to worship him. King Herod was deeply disturbed when he heard this" (Matthew 2:11). When they arrive, Jesus is a young child. They should have sent gifts by FedEx Next Day delivery.

The night before the first Christmas only three Wise Men were ready; everyone else was too busy to notice. The players and places have changed, but little else. We're urged to buy gifts until the night before finds most exhausted and in debt, with little thought of the importance. Will we join the crowd or be as wise men who saw His star

The night before and came to worship him?

Made in the USA
Middletown, DE
07 December 2018